"Every stepmom who is smart will read this book."

Drs. Les & Leslie Parrott
Founders of *RealRelationships.com*
Authors of *Love Talk*

"Ron Deal and Laura Petherbridge are two of America's top experts in the field of stepparenting and the blended family. This book brings you their very significant and helpful insight. I appreciate the positive and hopeful look at how to thrive and even flourish in the world of stepparenting."

Jim Burns
PhD, President of HomeWord
Author of *Confident Parenting,*
Creating an Intimate Marriage, and
Teaching Your Children Healthy Sexuality

"I can relate to so many of the testimonies that were given by women. This is a great book for every stepmom."

Paula Ward
MEd, LPC, LPC-S, LMFT, CDVC
Stepmom & Director of Guidance
and Counseling, Amarillo Independent
School District

"The Smart Stepmom by Ron L. Deal and Laura Petherbridge proves that a stepmom can not only survive, but thrive. Packed with lots of 'been there, lived that' guidance, the authors provide honest insight for day-to-day struggles. Each chapter concludes with a heartfelt prayer directed toward the specific challenges facing today's stepmom."

Ivey Harrington Beckman
Stepmom & Editor in Chief of
HomeLife magazine

"This book offers the tools and tips every stepmom needs to carry on with love, strength and a positive outlook. I recommend it for every woman who is entering the new life of stepparenting."

Karol Ladd
Author of *The Power of a Positive Mom*

"This book is rich with coaching on juggling the roles and opportunities as well as navigating the speed bumps that stepmoms experience day in and day out. Read it and pass it on to the stepmothers in your life. You will be thanked over and over again!"

Dr. Gary and Barb Rosberg
America's Family Coaches
Authors of 6 *Secrets to a Lasting Love,*
Radio show co-hosts and speakers
TheGreatMarriageExperience.com

"I would definitely recommend this book to anyone considering the stepmother role or anyone in that role already. I wish that I had read this book prior to my remarriage."

Diane, stepmom

"Simply put, the book is GREAT! I have learned so much that I can implement in my life. And there are lots of things that my husband may benefit from also."

Becky, stepmom of adult stepchildren
ages 28, 26, 24

The Smart Stepmom

Ron L. Deal &
Laura Petherbridge

BETHANYHOUSE
Minneapolis, Minnesota

Published by Bethany House Publishers
11400 Hampshire Avenue South
Bloomington, Minnesota 55438

Bethany House Publishers is a division of
Baker Publishing Group,
Grand Rapids, Michigan.

Printed in the United States of America

In keeping with biblical principles of creation stewardship, Baker Publishing Group advocates the responsible use of our natural resources. As a member of the Green Press Initiative, our company uses recycled paper when possible. The text paper of this book is comprised of 30% post-consumer waste.

green press INITIATIVE

Library of Congress Cataloging-in-Publication Data

Deal, Ron L.

The smart stepmom : practical steps to help you thrive! / by Ron L. Deal and Laura Petherbridge.
    p. cm.
Includes bibliographical references.
Summary: "Encouragement and practical advice for stepmoms on how to deal with their role in the stepfamily. Includes parenting advice, chapters for the husband to read, guidance for women dating men with children, and tips for relating to adult stepchildren"—Provided by publisher.
    ISBN 978-0-7642-0702-0 (pbk. : alk. paper)
    1. Stepmothers. 2. Remarried people—Family relationships. I. Petherbridge, Laura. II. Title.
    HQ759.92.D42   2009
    306.874'7—dc22

2009025244

DEDICATION

*To my mother: Your presence is and has always been a warm
blanket of love. Thank you.*

*And to all the stepmoms who shared their struggles, joys,
and hopes with us—this book is for you.*

Thank you for choosing to love.

—Ron

To my stepsons, Scott and Todd.

We have traveled this journey together.

For the times I was a wonderful stepmom—give God all the glory.

For the times I was a wicked stepmother—please forgive me.

—Laura

Books by
Ron L. Deal

Dating and the Single Parent

The Remarriage Checkup (with David H. Olson)

The Smart Stepdad

The Smart Stepfamily

The Smart Stepfamily Small Group Resource (DVD)

The Smart Stepmom (with Laura Petherbridge)

ACKNOWLEDGMENTS

Ron

    *I cannot write a book without support. If it weren't for my **loving children**, Braden, Connor, and Brennan, and **encouraging wife**, Nan, there's no way this project would have happened. I am truly grateful for your support through the years and am humbled by your love.*

    *This project is fortunate to have **Laura Petherbridge** as coauthor. I am so grateful for her writing skills, guidance, and wisdom. This book wouldn't be as practical or compelling without her contribution.*

    *In addition, this book stands on the shoulders of **thousands of stepmoms** who have shared their struggles, victories, and hopes with us through the years. Your transparency will help countless other stepmoms. Thank you.*

    *And finally, much thanks to the **Amarillo South Church** for supporting my efforts to strengthen stepfamilies throughout the world.*

Laura

A special thanks to:

***My friend and author Eva Marie Everson,** you saw my potential and "showed me the ropes."*

***The ladies in my writers' group:** Donna, Gloria, Laurie, LeAnne,*

Nicole, and Ruth. God used you to teach me how to write. You are true friends who have loved me in good times and bad.

My prayer team: Without you I'd be writing and speaking on my own strength—not a pretty picture.

My Web designer, Joanne Sample: You make my life so much easier and more colorful.

Sister stepmoms: You shared your pain and your passion, which made this book relevant for today's issues. I'm so grateful.

Ron Deal, my friend and coauthor: I appreciate your huge heart for stepfamilies. Thanks for your confidence that we would make a good team on this project.

My precious husband, Steve: There is no one I'd rather be married to. You love me, and believe in me, like no one else.

My Savior, Jesus Christ: You are the reason I breathe.

From both of us:

Thanks to **Kyle Duncan** and **Bethany House Publishers**. We are grateful for your heart and vision for a group of books for stepfamilies. Thank you for paving the way to hope for so many throughout the world. A special thank-you to our editor, **Ellen Chalifoux**—you make us look good!

To our agents, **Chip MacGregor** and **Wendy Lawton**: We appreciate your knowledge, hard work, patience, and friendship.

Contents

Section One: The Smart Stepmom: Who Is She?

Introduction   13

Chapter 1: Can You Hear Me Now?   19

Chapter 2: Can I Run Away From Home?   33

Chapter 3: The Wicked Stepmother: Did Disney Have Me in Mind?   51

Chapter 4: Understanding His Kids (Part 1): Loss, Grief, and Troubling Emotions   65

Chapter 5: Understanding His Kids (Part 2): Loyalty   83

Chapter 6: Partnering: Stepparenting Beside the Engaged or Disengaged Father   102

Section Two: Getting Smart: The Stepparenting Team

Chapter 7: Dad Smart (Part 1): She Can't Do It Without You   125

Chapter 8: Dad Smart (Part 2): Pitfalls and Good Intentions   140

Chapter 9: Meet Your Ex-Wife-in-Law: Friend or Foe?   155

Chapter 10: Understanding Your Kids: What Do They Need?   176

Chapter 11: Kodak Moments: Vacations, Holidays, Mother's Day, and Special Occasions   194

Chapter 12: Adult Stepchildren   216

Chapter 13: Baby Steps: Should We Have an "Ours" Baby?   241

Chapter 14: Smart Love   256

The Smart Stepmom: Who Is She?

INTRODUCTION

A counselor I (Ron) know opened a small envelope that arrived in his daily mail. The return address on the envelope and the Hallmark logo on the back told him it was a greeting card from former clients. Karen and Bill,[1] a stepfamily couple each with two children from previous relationships, had been married about six years. The couple initially came to therapy because Karen felt lonely and completely powerless in her home. "My husband's ex-wife has more influence over what goes on in my home than I do," she said in the first session. "Bill is caught between me, his kids, and his ex; I just don't have a place. We've been married six years, and I still feel so small in this family."

The counselor spent a number of sessions with the couple and their children working through issues. Karen seemed more optimistic about their future. The onset of summer brought added busyness to the couple so their counselor hadn't heard from them in a while. He was pleased to receive the greeting card and was eager to catch up on how they were doing. He opened the envelope. The front of the card read "With Special Thanks."

That's a good sign, he thought. *Things must be going pretty well.* He turned to the inside of the card and began reading. "I just wanted to thank you for trying to help me and Bill in our marriage. Unfortunately I have filed for divorce. . . ." *What?* he thought. *What happened to cause this downward turn?* He called Karen and she explained. Stress had taken its toll, her husband was even less willing than before to support her role as stepmom, and her own children were showing signs of distress. She had lost hope. "It's just so difficult being a stepmom," she said. "I tried so hard not to get to this point. I'm tired, and I just don't know what else to do. I'm going back to being a single mom."

We don't want this to happen to you.

One estimate suggests that the stepfamily will soon become (if it isn't already) the most common family form in America,[2] and one conservative estimate suggests that there are between eleven and eighteen million stepmothers of children under the age of eighteen in the U.S.[3] Despite this prevalence, stepmothers don't have a role model and often feel insignificant to their family. Peace, for many stepmothers, is ever elusive.

I (Ron) have been working with couples and families as a therapist and family educator for more than two decades. When I started speaking and writing specifically about the needs of stepfamilies in 1997, I had no idea how hungry stepfamily couples were for practical guidance. Due to the positive response, I began speaking around the country on a regular basis, started *SuccessfulStepfamilies.com*, conducted media interviews whenever I could, and wrote my first book, entitled *The Smart Stepfamily: Seven Steps to a Healthy Family*. I wanted stepfamilies to get smarter so they could beat the odds of divorce and find peace.

Today, through book and video resources, Web articles, a free monthly e-magazine, and marriage therapy intensives, Successful Stepfamilies is touching the lives of thousands on a regular basis. Yet despite these efforts, emails from around the world and stories about well-intentioned people like Karen taught me that our efforts were not enough. We had to do more.

Determined to offer more guidance, I again approached Bethany House Publishers with the idea to follow up *The Smart Stepfamily* with several more books for stepfamilies; they agreed. This first book is for you—the stepmom. Partnering with me on this project is my friend and co-champion for stepmoms, Laura Petherbridge. She is a divorce recovery expert featured on the DivorceCare DVD series that has equipped over 12,000 churches around the world, and she's also the author of *When "I Do" Becomes "I Don't": Practical Steps for Healing During Separation and Divorce*. A professional speaker, Laura conducts seminars on women's issues, divorce prevention, and spiritual growth. She has helped thousands of people walk through the transitions associated with divorce and remarriage. However, it's her personal credentials that make her the perfect coauthor for this book. As a child Laura experienced the trauma of her parents' divorce and later became a stepdaughter—twice. As an adult she has survived a divorce and has been a stepmother of two since 1985. Speaking as someone who has "been there, is doing that," she brings much-needed practical insight and life-chiseled wisdom to this Smart Stepmom resource.

I FEEL SO ALONE

Each member of a stepfamily deserves attention and support, but as I listened to the voices of various stepfamily members speaking to me over the years, the one voice that has shouted for help louder than all the others is that of the stepmom. Ghastly images of wicked stepmothers still shape our social milieu; even though unfair, such judgments also haunt the consciences of stepmoms who struggle to love their husbands and find their place with young and adult stepchildren alike. Karen, for example, felt alone in her stepfamily and overwhelmed by family dynamics she had no control over. In the end she decided that the only way to get her sanity back was to divorce her husband. Continuing to slowly press on as a stepmother just didn't seem like much of a future.

But stepmothers don't have to be alone, and they don't have to fall forward on shaky ground. With the proper perspective and tools, stepmothers can find solid ground on which to step.

In her Smart Stepmom seminars, Laura shares the unique reasons why stepmoms struggle to fit into the lives of stepchildren. She also provides insight on how to overcome the loneliness, fear, and frustration often associated with being a stepmother. Laura explains, "I foolishly assumed that because I grew up having two stepmothers I would automatically know how to be one. I was wrong. The job was much more complex than I imagined. But as I began to pray and ask God to teach me how to influence my stepchildren in a godly way, he infused my mind and heart with his compassion and grace. This provided the wisdom and support I often needed. My greatest desire was to find a resource and a support system with other stepmoms who understood the journey, but I never found one. That's why I was thrilled to hear of this project. Now other stepmoms will have what I've been seeking."

BECOMING A SMART STEPMOM

This book is designed to take you from surviving to thriving. We will explore why being a stepmom is, in our opinion, the most difficult role in the family today, and we'll give you a hopeful perspective that will defeat that occasional temptation to run away and never come back. And we'll tell you how not to be "wicked," despite what his children and ex-wife think.

As a stepparent you need to understand his children, so we'll also teach you how their past influences who they are and what you can do to help. We'll discuss the roles both you and your husband must play in order for you to be successful as a stepmom, and we've even included two chapters for your husband to read so he'll know how to elevate your status in the home. For those whose husband has an ex-wife, we'll show you how to increase cooperation between your homes. If you have children of your own, we'll tell you how to care for them so they don't get lost in the stepfamily shuffle. And in our effort to help you become a Smart Stepmom, we discuss vacations, holidays, relating to adult stepchildren, having an "ours" baby, and unique issues when the biological mother is deceased.

Over the years it has been our honor to walk with many women through the transition of becoming a stepmother, the ambiguity of a hard-to-define role, and the roller coaster of emotions that characterizes the typical stepmom experience. Recently Holly, a stepmother of three teenage stepdaughters, updated us on her stepfamily experience. She didn't start out a Smart Stepmom, but she learned how to become one.

Holly was hesitant about her role in the beginning. But to her credit, she latched on to some key concepts from one of our seminars and put them to work. Trying not to push her way into the hearts and lives of her stepdaughters, she let the girls take the lead in the type of relationship that would develop between them. Things started slowly, but eventually each of the girls invited her into their activities and then into their hearts. She wisely chose to respond slowly with discipline and punishment when the girls made a poor choice. Holly allowed her husband to remain the primary parent during the early years of their stepfamily. When the girls' biological mother, who had been distant and uninvolved for a few years, decided to take a more active role, Holly adjusted her expectations and didn't compete. Paradoxically, this willingness to serve brought a great return on her investment.

The obvious payoff came during a "family anniversary," which Holly shared with us. "Our anniversary was a moment of victory for our family. Mike and I wanted to include his girls, now seventeen, fourteen, and twelve, in the celebration, so I ordered a replica of the top layer of our wedding cake. After church we gathered around the kitchen table eating cake and toasting our marriage with glasses of milk. Mike and I told the girls the story of how we met, some of our dating adventures, and even funny things that happened on our honeymoon. Then we reminisced about the wedding and reminded the girls of their part in the ceremony. There was a lot of laughter. What a wonderful evening it was. Even the girls shared their fondest memories of our family. At one point the oldest said, 'It's our anniversary too, you know!' "

Holly went on to explain that not every moment in her family is this satisfying. "Over the years I've had to redefine my role with the girls. At times it's been difficult and hurtful, but I've learned to press through those moments. As for Mike and I, we are doing great! We would not have made it this far, with this many successes, had it not been for you. Thanks so much."

Holly's trek as a stepmom has been full of peaks, valleys, and moments where she couldn't find the map. We suspect your journey will be too. An ending similar to Holly's may feel unrealistic or unobtainable for your situation, but we encourage you to hang on because this book is designed to offer insight on how to sustain hope in the valleys and prolonged time on the peaks. Take these steps and we are confident that you—like Holly—will become a Smart Stepmom.

Chapter 1

Can You Hear Me Now?

I (Laura) turned on my home computer and headed to the kitchen for a cup of coffee as I attempted to wake up. Steaming cup in hand and now resting in the comfortable chair, my eyes tried to focus on the flurry of activity on the screen. My inbox was going into cardiac arrest! Now fully awake, I watched the arriving messages pour in—thirty, forty, fifty, and still climbing. There was no end in sight. What in the world was happening? Glancing at the subject line I noticed a recurring word—Stepmom!

Stepmothers from everywhere were sending me their thoughts in response to a few sentences that my coauthor, Ron, had posted on his stepfamily e-magazine. I was seeking the top five issues facing today's stepmothers, and he had listed my email address for feedback. Hence the tidal wave of responses.

After reading each letter, a resounding message came through loud and clear. The stepmoms who wrote to me were deeply hurting. They felt isolated and didn't know where to find help. Many of them attended churches that offer information on marriage, but the topics typically focused on gender differences, communication skills, and marital intimacy. Although those were helpful, they didn't address the extreme pain, frustration, or unique issues associated with stepfamilies.

I've been a stepmom since 1985, and I understand the loneliness and confusion I read in their notes. After a very painful divorce I met my present husband, Steve, who had been single for eight years. His two sons from his first marriage were eleven and thirteen when we married, and they didn't want or need a stepmother. My husband and I were clueless about dealing with the whole situation.

During my childhood and adult years I had had two stepmothers myself. My dad remarried twice after he was divorced from my mother. I foolishly assumed this experience prepared me for *becoming* a stepmother. I was wrong.

In the letters I received, a number of the marriages were on the verge of divorce. None of the women desired for their marriages to end, but the relationships were dying. Some of the most prevalent reasons included verbally and physically abusive stepkids, a manipulative former wife, intolerant in-laws, cruelty to her own biological children by stepsiblings or the stepdad, increasing debt, and husbands who wouldn't take steps toward helping the marriage survive, much less thrive.

Ron and I understand that in order to provide relief for stepmoms, we must be realistic. We can't tackle the complex issues associated with being a stepmom if we sugarcoat the problems. To quote TV psychologist Dr. Phil McGraw, "You can't change what you won't acknowledge." The Bible says it this way: "A prudent [or wise] man sees danger and takes refuge, but the simple keep going and suffer for it" (Proverbs 22:3).

So let's begin by taking an honest look at the challenges. Consider these statements from fellow stepmoms:

I didn't realize that a second marriage would cause me to give up the dream of a perfect or whole family. Everyone's illusions change after marriage, but it's particularly difficult when children and a former spouse are involved.

Even though the role of being a mother hasn't been easy, being a stepmom has been a thousand times more difficult and painful.

There aren't a lot of positives associated with being second. Society says second place, second best—secondhand isn't good enough.

In the early days of my marriage I believed my husband when he said his former wife was unloving and a bad mom. But now I've realized that he has played a role in the problems.

Even fairy tales portray the second wife as the villain; she is always the "wicked stepmother."

Neither my husband nor his former wife is willing to give up the dance of bitterness and revenge.

How am I to believe that my husband loves me when he refuses to stand up to his children when they treat me with disrespect? I am his wife.

I wouldn't wish this experience on anyone. It's extremely hard for the children and the new wife.

Is there any hope? Absolutely. Listen to Lynn's story—a journey to victory—submitted on Ron's Web page.

Lynn and her husband combined six children—ages three, four, five, six, eight, and ten—who lived with them full time because her ex-husband was an alcoholic and his ex-wife abandoned her children. She faced typical challenges when her stepchildren minimized her authority ("You're not our mom!") and remained loyal to a biological mother they didn't know. When her stepchildren reached adolescence, their mother reappeared and instantly turned them further against Lynn. Despite the fact that the biological mom had been absent for many years, she still had the power to tear apart everything that Lynn had built with her stepkids. Disrespect and conflict became a daily occurrence in Lynn's home, and her husband didn't handle his children well. Their marriage was in turmoil to the point that Lynn wanted a divorce. But she didn't file. The dream of growing old together kept her from leaving and eventually produced fruit she never imagined.

When her second-oldest stepson was about to enter the Iraq War, he used his allotted two hours of phone time not to call his biological mother or father, but his stepmother, Lynn. He apologized to her for his prior behavior and thanked her for offering discipline and guidance throughout his life. He especially thanked her for raising him to know the Lord. "After that call," she wrote, "I knew that every minute of being a stepmom was worth it. We've now survived fifteen years of marriage, five high school graduations, one college graduation, three USMC boot camp graduations, and two weddings, and now we have two granddaughters. So, to all stepmoms out there, hang in there. You'll survive too." And we think you can thrive!

Learning to thrive begins by acknowledging and understanding the complex issues associated with stepfamilies and then applying smart stepfamily solutions.

A Smart Stepmom:

- doesn't pretend that a second marriage is the same as a first, and she doesn't expect everyone to be happy.
- acknowledges that it's normal to love stepchildren differently than biological kids.

- discovers the things she can control and releases the things she can't.

- understands the vast difference between enabling and mercy. She knows that healthy boundaries are often necessary to create stability.

- has educated herself about normal stepfamily development and uses that understanding to make sense of her current relationships and circumstances.

- takes the time to understand children who are coping with loss and loyalty conflicts. Her goal is to ease the grief whenever possible rather than create more chaos.

- recognizes that children often feel disloyal to the biological mom if they treat their stepmom kindly.

- doesn't step hastily into her husband's parenting role, even when he refuses to do so.

- respectfully discusses issues about the children privately with her husband.

- learns when and how to address conflict in her marriage and with her stepchildren and her extended stepfamily.

- is constantly growing and learning about wise stepparenting and parenting strategies.

- is prepared. She isn't naïve or ambushed by complex stepfamily issues and is flexible to cope with matters that she didn't see coming.

- has a strong support system with other women who share her values.

- tries to be at peace with the biological mom and asks God to help her see things from the biological mom's viewpoint.

- does not try to become a replacement mother to children who already have one, nor does she insist that the children call her Mom.

- recognizes that there are limits to her contribution to decision-making regarding her stepchildren's lives (examples could include choice of physician, educational environment, or wedding planning, etc.).

- accepts that sometimes being a stepmother is going to be unfair and lonely.

- uses God's standards as her guidelines for life.

- knows that God can and will give her a supernatural love for her husband's children if she sincerely asks.

- acknowledges that she may not see the fruit of her sacrifices until the children become adults.

- resists the negative label associated with being a stepmother.

- believes her value is determined by the price Jesus paid for her and that she is precious in God's eyes. This awareness offers her enduring peace even in challenging circumstances.

If you are like most women, while reading this list you graded yourself by checking off which descriptions you currently portray and which you do not. Don't be discouraged. These points—and others throughout the book—represent direction for you as a stepmom, and the quotes throughout the chapters are reminders that you are not alone. This list of Smart Stepmom qualities represents hope for the future. With confidence you can learn solutions that strengthen a marriage and bring peace to your spirit. This process takes time and patience. Moving from surviving to thriving doesn't happen overnight, but it can be done.

A Personal Prescription

Every stepfamily is different. It would be impossible for us to address each individual circumstance. But throughout this book we attempt to address as many different stepmom circumstances as possible. Occasionally you will note a sidebar that addresses a specific issue such as dating a man with children, part-time stepmoms, situations where the biological mother is deceased, or stepmothers with adult stepchildren. Be sure to read the sidebars that apply most to you.

SMART STEPS (FOR STEPMOMS)

While every stepmom situation is different, there are some foundational principles of successful stepfamily living that Smart Stepmoms embrace. In Ron's book *The Smart Stepfamily,* he discusses crucial steps necessary to building a strong stepfamily. These key steps lay a foundation for the remainder of this book; therefore, we are reviewing them here. If you read that book, don't skip this section, as this review is written from a stepmom's perspective and highlights how each step specifically relates to her place in the home.

How to Cook a Stepfamily

Perhaps you enjoy cooking. In the kitchen of your stepfamily's heart there are a number of ingredients (that is, people). Some have a tough exterior, some are soft; some are spicy, and some are relatively bland. The "cooking method" you use to combine the ingredients of your home is very important. The wrong cooking method can result in a mess; the best cooking method makes an enjoyable meal possible.

Stepmoms who use the *blender* cooking method often ruin the family meal. A classic example is the stepmom who insists her stepkids instantly call her Mom. She has good intentions, but trying to force "a good blend" of ingredients can inadvertently cause friction.

Smart stepmoms know the wisest way to cook a stepfamily is with a Crockpot. Slow cookers, as they are sometimes called, utilize *time* and *low heat* in the cooking process, instead of the high friction of a blender. Imagine you are cooking stew for dinner. You throw beef, carrots, potatoes, tomatoes, celery, and onions into the

Crockpot, and place the lid on. It takes quite a while for the low heat to begin generating enough warmth to soften all the ingredients. Serving the stew after just thirty minutes is not wise. The carrots and potatoes aren't soft, the juices of the ingredients haven't begun to mix, and the undercooked beef is dangerous for consumption. But wait six or seven hours, and the ingredients have softened and combined into something really delicious.

The natural cooking time of stepfamilies is slow, and it may take many years before ingredients soften. So while you're waiting for your family to fully cook, discover the normal process of development and be patient with the results.

Step Down Your Expectations

Crockpot cooking means letting go of expectations, especially those that are oriented around time and the depth of the relationship with your stepchildren. Understand that you will never become *the real mom* to your stepchildren. As a stepmom you may hold a unique and special place in their hearts, but you will never be Mom. There is only one God-given mother in each of our lives. Give yourself a break. You cannot take her place, so don't go crazy trying.

Relaxing about your performance as a stepmother is a challenge. This is largely due to the societal pressure placed on women to be the focal point for family closeness, emotional connection, and socialization of the children. One writer calls this the motherhood mandate.[1] It assumes that women should define themselves in light of family relationships and will, therefore, care for family members to the best of their ability. Without even realizing it, women often organize their thoughts, feelings, and behaviors around the role of motherhood.

Stepmothers are often asked to carry a similar weight of responsibility for their stepchildren. Frequently they are asked by their husbands and society to be responsible for the quality of relationships within the home and the well-being of the children. A stepmother who accepts this responsibility often judges herself a "good mother," which is rewarding, or a "bad mother," which leads to guilt. Further, stepmothers who more closely identify with their spousal role than parental role (*mothering but not a mother*) may fear being judged uncaring or wicked by friends, neighbors, or family members.[2]

All of this pressure to perform—what we might call the *stepmother mandate*—creates tremendous stress and guilt for some stepmoms. Stepmothers often fail to recognize that they don't have the same emotional attachment, influence, or power within the home to bring about "good mothering." You aren't *the* mother, so how can you successfully mother?

Whether stemming from your own internal pressure, family members, friends, or society in general, combating the stepmother mandate begins with understanding that cooking a stepfamily is not entirely your responsibility, nor do you possess enough influence to make it happen exactly as you desire. Crockpot cooking is a process that is influenced by every family member and the dynamics between them. Instead of taking on the burden of being the focal point for the relationships within your family, only accept responsibility for your part. Allow others to accept theirs.

Two Step—Make Your Marriage a Priority

Making your marriage a priority means developing a healthy marital relationship. Not long ago Dr. David Olson and I (Ron) conducted the largest qualitative study of couples creating stepfamilies to discover the qualities of a healthy stepfamily marriage. Our findings are published in a book called *The Remarriage Checkup*. In brief, we discovered that the top five predictors of healthy, vibrant stepfamily marriages are:

1. *Personality Compatibility*—Healthy couples are comprised of healthy individuals who are not controlling, jealous, angry,

Step Money

How many checking or savings accounts couples put money into does not seem to make a significant difference in couple satisfaction with money management.[3] What does matter is that the couple agrees to the solution and shares values about spending, saving, and giving, and how money is used to care for family members.

moody, or overly critical. In addition we found that the presence of fear (e.g., of another relationship breakup) was extremely defeating to the marriage, while confidence and trust increased marital intimacy.

2. *Healthy Communication*—Like oil in an engine, good communication skills ensure that the working parts of your marriage don't encounter too much friction. Every couple occasionally miscommunicates, but healthy couples really work at talking, listening, and understanding each other.

3. *Conflict Resolution*—Disagreements can create a fire that destroys your marriage, or they can help your marriage grow by burning up the unwanted parts of your relationship. The goal should be to manage conflict in a healthy manner.

4. *Leisure Time Together*—What we sometimes called the "fun factor" of a great remarriage, this quality speaks to whether you and your husband have regular, frequent leisurely time together. Notice that this isn't about each of you having individual leisure time, rather fun time spent together. Enjoying a nightly walk or occasional date out on the town, playing cards or tennis, or any other activity that is shared contributes to a satisfying marriage.

5. *Couple Flexibility*—This describes your ability to adapt and change to life's circumstances. Couples with rigid attitudes often find themselves stuck, not knowing how to resolve stepfamily dilemmas. In addition, they are at odds with each other much more frequently than those who work together to manage the family's schedule, time demands, and decisions.

Building these qualities in your marriage should be a priority for you and your husband. Together they alone predict with over

98 percent accuracy whether a remarried couple will have a strong marriage or a poor one.[4] Commit to working on these areas, and your family will benefit.

Step in Line With the Parenting Team

Stepfamily parenting has two key aspects: parenting with the adults in the other home and parenting as a father-stepmother team. Those with children moving between two (or more) homes know how challenging cooperation with ex-spouses can be. Healthy co-parenting focuses on putting aside the differences you have with an ex-spouse (or husband's ex-spouse) and cooperating on matters regarding the children's well-being. This is always easier said than done.

We like to say that your husband's ex-wife is your ex-wife-in-law. You never chose her as a relative, but she is one. To parent effectively you have to establish a workable relationship with her (whether she deserves it or not). We'll devote an entire chapter to this matter later in the book, but for now, realize that your relationship with her has a great impact on your family.

> ### Get a Relationship Checkup
>
> Invite your boyfriend or husband to take the online Couple Checkup with you at *www.SuccessfulStepfamilies.com* (for dating, engaged, and married couples). An objective scientific analysis helps motivate men to work on their relationship.

Working together as a father-stepmother team is also important. Several chapters in this book outline how you and your husband can accomplish this as well as offer guidance for empty-nest stepmothers, but one critical principle to mention here is that authority is based on relationship. Wise stepmothers build a warm, trusting relationship with stepchildren before trying to become a parental authority. The road to being labeled *wicked* is paved with demanding obedience from children who don't know or trust your heart. Once they know that you care, then and only then have you earned the right to lead and discipline.

When Mom Is Deceased

Expect your stepchildren to have a measure of loyalty to how their mother did and might have parented them. One eleven-year-old told his father, "If you get married to her and she changes the rules, I'll follow Mom's rules instead."

- Try to know what kind of parent their mother was and what she valued. Since you stand in her shadow, this will help you understand how your stepchildren experience you.
- Compliment their mother's values and parenting when you can. She is not your enemy.
- Some children feel confused about embracing your love. Letting you in may make them feel like they're losing Mom again. Be patient with what appear to be hot/cold responses, and think of it as confusion instead.

REAL-LIFE WISDOM

This book is drawn in part from our years of experience in training individuals and families, conducting stepfamily coaching and therapy, and conducting solid social research on healthy stepfamily living. In addition, we want you to know that we are Christians and speak from our faith perspective. Because our faith and research converge in a powerful way, we believe the principles in this resource apply to anyone searching for insight on becoming a Smart Stepmom. You don't have to share our faith to gain practical strength from this book.

Finally, to assist you with practical implementation, we have concluded each chapter with questions. These can be used individually, in discussion with your husband, or as part of a stepmoms support group. We strongly encourage you to connect with other stepmoms to share your journey. There *is* strength in numbers. Because we know stepmoms often need encouragement, we have also included thoughtful prayers and relevant Bible passages at the close of each chapter as a source of comfort and strength.

So grab a cup of coffee, chai tea, or a Coke, and let's move forward.

PRAYER

Lord, the desire of my heart is to become a Smart Stepmom. The Bible tells me that you are the way and the truth and the meaning of all life. And that you came to give me an abundant life filled with your goodness. Thank you that I can bring my weariness and heavy burdens to you, and that you promise to replace them with peace and rest for my soul.

I want to finish this life with confidence that I have done my part in seeking your wisdom and insight every step of the way. Help me to keep my emotions or misguided thinking in check. I love you, Lord. And I seek your face. Open my heart that I might see and hear you more clearly. Your guidance makes my eyes light up and brings joy into my life.

PRAYER REFERENCES

John 3:16　　　　　　　　*2 Corinthians 1:12*
John 10:10　　　　　　　 *Proverbs 14:12*
Matthew 11:28–30　　　　*Psalm 19:8*

Smart Stepmom Discussion Questions

1. How long have you been a stepmom, or where are you in the process right now?

2. What has surprised you the most about becoming a stepmom?

3. What was your reaction to the quotes from other stepmoms? Is there one that sounds like you?

4. What are the best parts/worst parts of being a stepmom for you?

5. What is your relationship with your stepchildren at this point? If you could improve in one area, what would it be?

6. Reviewing the Smart Stepmom list, what are the top three areas you feel need the most attention?

7. Does knowing that your feelings and frustrations are common among stepmoms help with the anger, loneliness, or isolation?

8. What is discouraging and what is a relief about learning that step-families often take a number of years to "cook"?

9. Which of the following best describes how far along your family is in the Crockpot?

   • Ingredients still separated (before the wedding)
   • Just put the lid on (newlyweds)
   • Beginning to warm (the early years)
   • Some softening (indications of developing emotional connection)
   • Juices are sharing (combining of two or more ingredients to different degrees)
   • Stew! (tastes good for the most part)

10. What significant outcome would you like to see as a result of reading this book?

Chapter 2

Can I Run Away From Home?

There have been many times as a stepmom when I (Laura) felt like running away from home. The loneliness and frustration often felt overwhelming, and no one seemed to understand. In the earlier years of my second marriage I'd stomp around like a three-year-old demanding that God do something. I wanted a "normal" marriage, with "normal" problems. Then shame and guilt would consume me for my immaturity, and I'd emotionally pummel myself for being self-centered. It was a never-ending battle. I hated what I was becoming. Crumpling into a chair I'd pray, "Lord, I need you to teach me how to survive this marriage and love my stepkids, because left to my own devices, it's going to get ugly around here." Fortunately, he loves honesty.

FEELING LIKE AN OUTSIDER

For many stepmoms the pain goes soul deep. When we asked a group of stepmoms why they wanted to run away from home, four responses came back repeatedly.

"I feel like a stranger in my own home."

When his kids come to our home, it is uncomfortable for everyone. My husband and I go from being a couple to being separate. This causes me such loneliness and I feel like a stranger in my own home.

———

After the wedding we moved into his house and agreed to put my things in the basement. I didn't realize that living among someone else's stuff can make you feel like a stranger. I would go to the basement and lie on my old beat-up couch because it was so wonderful to feel like home.

———

I traveled to a foreign country many years ago, and my own home now reminds me of the isolation I felt there.

———

My husband and his kids laugh and reminisce over old times, while my kids and I sit on the sidelines. We have discussed this many times but he feels that they should "have him"'on the weekends.

———

My husband and his daughters have such a strong bond that I will never be a part of, and it makes me feel like an outsider in my own home.

———

My husband is a different man when his kids arrive. And my own children wonder, "Where did my normal stepdad go?"

Smart Dating

If you are still dating, you may find the feelings expressed in this section foreign. We encourage you to read it anyway to help you anticipate what may happen to you at some point. These feelings are not universal, but to varying intensities, common.

"I live in constant fear, and the only place I feel safe is in my bedroom."

The atmosphere of my house changes as soon as the stepkids arrive. I don't feel safe.

We're polite to each other, but we know there is a big pink elephant in the room.

———

It is like being in a Mafia setting. I have to constantly watch my words for fear they will be misinterpreted. I am not allowed to have an opinion, good or bad, about anything.

———

I have to make sure all my personal things are either hidden or locked away when the stepkids visit.

———

When my stepdaughter left for an extended vacation, I realized how imprisoned I felt in my own home. The tension and fear of doing the wrong thing or being hurt by her ugly actions was gone. It was my home again.

———

When his daughters visit I keep to myself; when they are not around I am able to "walk about the cabin freely."

———

I feel so alone, and I live in fear of saying the wrong thing or being hurt by vindictive actions or words.

———

I watch every word I say, knowing it will be repeated to his former wife as soon as the kids return home.

"A sense of dread fills me when I come home."

I hate my house when his kids come over. I have to shift into survival mode.

———

When Mom Is Deceased

If you have moved into the home once occupied by your husband and his deceased wife, you may feel that her "ghost" is alive and well. Ideally, try to purchase a new house. If that is not possible, find small but significant ways of making the home yours. Realize that children will want to retain certain decorations or pictures that remind them of their mother. When reserved to their personal space (e.g., bedroom or bathroom), this is appropriate.

I dread coming home when I know the stepkids will be there.

———

The anxiety I feel when I pull into my driveway is the same as when I was married to an abusive husband.

———

All the rules change as soon as his kids arrive.

"I am a nobody in this house."

Much of the time I feel like I could be replaced by a housekeeper/cook and no one would know the difference.

———

My husband says there are rooms in our home that are off limits to me. When I can't stand the filth or smell anymore, he tells me to avoid those rooms.

———

His kids couldn't care less if I'm in the room; they totally ignore me.

———

I'm the second-class citizen in our home when my stepchildren are here.

———

I stand nowhere in the chain of command; I'm the third in charge—if that.

———

I am a nonentity in this home.

It's discouraging, isn't it? But for many it's a reality.

OVERCOMING

Are there ways a stepmom can overcome these feelings? The most successful
stories of victory result when the dad recognizes the situation and the two of you
conquer the problems together.

> My husband and I sat down with the
> kids and told them things were going to
> be different. Then we identified specific
> things families must do to maintain a
> loving and supportive home, such as
> sharing chores and feeling free to speak
> true feelings. We also made a written
> pact not to disrespect anyone in the
> home, which is posted throughout the
> house so it's always visible.

Smart Dating

Arguments that appear to be about money are often really about values. What we buy and how much we're willing to spend is determined by what we value. Learn all you can about your dating partner's financial history. Watch what he spends his money on and you'll have insight into his values. Keeping in mind that satisfied couples have similar values, ask yourself how his compare to yours.

However, you may be married to a man who has chosen not to
address the problems making your life more difficult. This chapter
will focus on what you can do to move forward.

Change the Nest

To help you feel more at home, consider making changes. It's
amazing how making the slightest changes to "his" home can help
some stepmoms feel like it's "ours." If either your husband or the
kids are resistant, begin gradually. Your own bedroom is a great
place to begin, and then expand from there as able.

> We started by changing our bedroom and bath. I picked out
> wallpaper, curtains, and a bedspread, which gave the room a
> whole new look. I bought matching towels, and we had at least
> one place that was a reflection of my own style. The bedroom
> and bathroom are off limits to the kids because I needed
> someplace we could call our own.

———

An understanding friend asked us to pick out the pattern for a quilt that she made as a wedding gift.

———

We painted the rooms in our house, and I picked all the colors. New countertops and wall hangings were blended with his furniture. Adding my touches around "his" stuff helped to make it "our" home. Now I love my house.

Encourage Dad to Have Alone Time With His Kids

After my (Laura) parents divorced and my dad remarried, the only time I had him to myself was the thirty-minute ride from my house to his. Once we arrived at his house he was busy doing other things. Now that I'm a stepmother myself, logic would say my childhood experience would have taught me to encourage my husband to have alone time with his sons, but somehow I missed it. One of the biggest mistakes I made as a stepmom was to underestimate the importance of his kids having their dad all to themselves. If I had it to do over again this would be the first item on the list.

> **Befriending Adult Stepchildren**
>
> Surprisingly, adult stepchildren really cherish time alone with their father just as younger children do. Don't underestimate the importance of time. It is your gift to them that invites respect and honor.

My husband and his kids have a lot of alone time . . . which alleviates my being an obstacle between them. We get season passes to nearby parks, and he often takes them for the whole day. At other times the kids spend time alone with their grandparents overnight.

The goal for providing exclusive time together is to make your time with them feel less intrusive. It also nurtures the bruised hearts of stepchildren who have lost their family, contact with both parents, and a sense of stability in their lives. These losses likely make them feel anxious about sharing their dad with you because it feels like yet another loss. Giving them time alone with their father often helps to soothe their fearful hearts.

Girlfriends and More Girlfriends

When I got married I made the mistake of losing contact with my friends. I was so ready for this marriage that I had no time for my friends. I now realize that was a special part of me that I forfeited for the sake of this marriage.

A big mistake women often make after finding the man of their dreams is to eliminate girlfriends. This is not just a stepmom issue. God is my provider, and he is the strong tower to which we run when life becomes frazzled and complicated (Proverbs 18:10); however, he often provides laughter, comfort, advice, and a hot fudge sundae to ease the pain through a much-needed girlfriend.

Stepmoms are frequently ambushed by foreign emotions causing them to wonder, *Who is this woman in the mirror?* Time laughing or crying with girlfriends can help to restore the inner person that still exists. A few hours with people who know me as "Laura" rather than "the wicked stepmother" helps to restore my personality.

To counter the feeling of getting swallowed up into the drama between my spouse and his kids, I spend quality time at the gym or visit friends and family. I am like a supporting actor in a story about his/their life. But when I am around my own family or friends, it reminds me of who I am and that I have value.

Take Baby Steps

You may be like me (Laura). I was raised to be polite to adults regardless of the circumstances. If my mother detected even a hint of cockiness in my tone of voice, much less body language, there was a severe consequence. Therefore, it is extremely hard for me to fathom a child ignoring or talking back to an adult. In my home this was absolutely forbidden. But times are different.

Many of the isolation issues stepmoms face are due to the fact that the children refuse to speak directly to her. They desire conversation with Dad—only Dad. She is left to ponder, *How do you build a relationship with someone who has no desire to converse? How do you hug a porcupine?* This is how one woman tackled the issue.

> *My counselor suggested that I start out small. At first my goal was to have one good interaction with them a day. I began by asking a question or giving a compliment. After I was successful with one per day, I moved it up to two and so on. They finally began to respond to my interest in them. It's not perfect, but it has gotten better.*

Her solution may rub you like sandpaper. My initial reaction was, "That's ridiculous. Why should an adult need to tiptoe around kids that way?" However, ask yourself this question: Do I want a harmonious home, or do I want to be right? Am I willing to take baby steps toward building a relationship with these kids, or am I going to be sequestered in my bedroom forever? Hiding is easier—that's for certain—but it doesn't solve the issues. This woman's response is a good illustration of the "low heat" Crockpot cooking method we discussed in chapter 1. Begin *where* you can, connect *when* you can, and over time ingredients will soften, making way for deeper connections.

Start New Traditions

> *I began our own scrapbook by taking pictures of events. It took time to establish our own memories. But now when my stepkids say, "Remember when we did this or that," I know I'm not the stranger anymore.*

This is not something that will work overnight, but it's a great place to start. As a stepmom of twenty-three years, I (Laura) now share a history of people, places, and things I can laugh about with my stepsons.

But remember, give your stepkids permission to have a past that doesn't include you. If you wish to join the conversation when your husband or stepkids mention a past memory, instead of retreating and allowing it to ostracize you, share something similar that you remember. It helps them to recognize that you had another life too.

> *If the kids talked about a holiday when they got a new doll, I would mention a time when I got a new doll. . . . Stepchildren are strangers to your past. Sharing former experiences helps to make the situation feel equal.*

Manage Your Emotions and Fears

I finally decided that this is my home too, and I never want to go back to feeling like the outsider.

When the tender feelings of rejection, estrangement, or isolation become overwhelming, most people respond with the more crass emotions of anger, bitterness, or resentment. These strong negative emotions usually express themselves as criticism, attacking words, or emotional distancing. The problem with this type of response is that it gives the very ones with whom you are trying to connect further reason to withhold themselves from you. The result is increased polarization and loneliness in your home, with both sides feeling justified in blaming the other.

So what can you do? Begin by finding the best time to work through difficult emotions with your husband. If your stepchildren, for example, spend time in another home, wait to discuss emotional issues until his kids are gone. This might make the conversation less reactive since the children aren't front and center. It also gives you uninterrupted time to have a focused conversation and resolve any issues.

Next, manage your negative emotions and fears so you can speak out of a desire for increased relationship and trust with your husband and stepchildren instead of speaking out of your hurt or resentment.

Stepmom Self-Care

Sharing your heart's desire with your stepchildren may or may not be wise. Wounded stepchildren might use your honesty to hurt you further. If you believe their character to be such, share these desires only with your husband.

- When overwhelmed with negative feelings, take an emotional break if necessary to process your emotions. If retreating to your bedroom for a short time or taking a walk around the block is the sanctuary you need, then do it. Examine your heart and ask God to reveal the root cause. For example, anger is a secondary emotion and always has a more important primary emotion—like hurt, frustration, or sadness—underneath. Look beyond the obvious anger to find what lies beneath.

- Share your heart's desire and the fear that goes with it with your spouse. "I know I get upset when all of you are telling stories that precede my joining the family. It's not that I dislike what you're doing. I just wish I could share in it with you. To be honest, I really want to be included and sometimes feel that I'm not. I long for a closer relationship with you; you mean that much to me. I apologize for getting upset earlier, and I'll try to control that better. Just know I really care for you and the kids."

- Let God soothe your fears. Making the above statement to people that you already fear don't accept you is incredibly difficult (maybe you felt anxious as you envisioned saying it). It risks being vulnerable with them even when you can't guarantee they will embrace you. To be honest, most people can't do it. They feel better hiding behind the walls of anger, criticism, and blame. But if you are going to soften the environment and encourage them to take you in, you must speak out of your desire for relationship with them, not your fear or self-protection. Ask God to soothe your heart in those moments and give you strength to love those who aren't yet as loving toward you as you'd like.

If He Won't Hear Your Pain

Sometimes your pain is ignored by your spouse and nothing seems to get his attention. That's when the desire to pull away is intense. One woman expressed the depth of her pain and her coping strategy this way: "I've not given up on my marriage. I pray each day that God will intervene . . . that he will help me somehow overcome the hurts that have been inflicted on me and help me to be a kinder person. But for now, disengaging is working for me."

Sometimes stepmoms find themselves in extremely challenging circumstances. You may have tried everything we've already mentioned, but your husband still won't hear you. It's possible he may help to improve things for a while but then slides back into old habits. You wonder how you can love more completely. You've extended yourself as much as possible and yet the children still treat you like an outsider; you are actively spoken against and treated with great disdain. And to make matters worse, your husband won't stand up for your place in the family. You are the easy target and no one is lacking for arrows. What can you do?

For many, emotionally disengaging seems to be a common coping strategy. But while this does provide some temporary relief from pain, over time it tends to increase your isolation, loneliness, and resentment. It's not a long-term solution.

Furthermore, setting boundaries in unhealthy relationships by simply emotionally disengaging often doesn't work for stepmoms. In biological families removing oneself from the situation creates emotional discomfort for the recipient that can motivate them to change their behavior. However, this may not be the result when you're the stepmom. Think about it. You are in pain because you are treated like an outsider. You feel as though you don't belong, and you aren't given the full respect of a parent or the consideration a wife deserves. If you emotionally disconnect, in effect saying,

"Fine. Since you treat me like an outsider, I'm going to become more of an outsider. That will teach you," you may be sabotaging yourself.

This is also true when stepmoms become overly critical and negative toward those they feel rejected by. You simply aren't as important to them as you want to be—which is why you feel like an outsider! Being negative probably won't ignite in them a motivation to change. If anything, it gives your stepchildren more justification for treating you as an outsider. An enemy can't claim the rights of an ally.

If this is your situation, you've got to try something different. You've got to try a love that balances boundaries with sacrifice.

Politely Resign. Every time Sandra tried to encourage her stepson to learn a skill or manage his responsibilities, he fought her authority. Ultimately Sandra's husband would get involved by criticizing her parenting and sabotaging everything she was trying to do. Sandra resigned. After carefully choosing her words, she tendered this resignation: "Tom, we continually battle over how to parent your son. We have discussed these issues many times, and we even verbally agree on a plan. But every time I try to implement the plan, you side against me. Since we really don't have an agreement, there's no reason for this pattern to continue. Therefore, I am resigning my post as person in charge of your son. For example, I will no longer be in charge of getting him out of bed in the morning and ready for school. Do not count on me to get this—or similar tasks—done. I'm not angry or doing this out of malice, but there will be less conflict for everyone if you handle it the way you desire."

Sandra then lived up to this declaration, leaving a number of gaps in the home structure. Her husband felt every one of them, and it opened his eyes. What Sandra didn't do—and this is very important—was to emotionally disengage from her husband or stepchildren. She resigned from the responsibilities and tasks (that she couldn't fulfill anyway), but she remained open to her family emotionally. She looked for opportunities to speak to and engage her stepchildren and continued to show respect and love to her husband.

Without playing emotional games, resigning shifts the weight of responsibility. The hope and goal is that someone else feel the weight and find motivation to change. In this case, Sandra felt the weight of being an authority in a system where she had no authority. She shifted that weight to her husband (the person who needed to own the problem), so he could deal with the consequences of his previous behavior.

If you take this action, it is very important to be polite and matter-of-fact in your message and actions. Do not be sarcastic or overly critical when carrying out your resignation. If you lecture at every turn ("See, it's not easy to get your son up in the morning, is it?"), this gives your husband reason to be angry with you. His focus needs to be on the problem, not you. Don't be mean-spirited, just resign. It's possible your spouse may become angry that your resignation has caused him to suffer a consequence. Above all, remain emotionally available and open to your family. This communicates your desire for greater relationship (as we discussed earlier) and openness to changes in the home.

> ## A Stepmom Who "Resigned"
>
> "Before we married, my husband's three girls ran him ragged. He enforced no discipline and they took advantage of it. For three years I tried to take over the discipline in our home, but it just resulted in more conflict. Because of your advice I stepped back completely and something amazing happened. My husband quit focusing on my parenting and noticed the discipline gaps for the first time. He started learning how to parent his girls—not because I told him to, but because he opened himself up to letting God change him. I've learned that things get done in God's time, not mine. If I step out, God can step in."

Redefine How You Will Love. Sometimes Christians have a self-serving view of wedding vows. We write about them, teach on them, and rightfully sermonize on why it is important that we uphold them throughout our marriage. And then, when someone files for divorce, we automatically blame them for breaking the wedding vows when many times, the vows were quietly broken by the other spouse. For example, when a man verbally denigrates his wife for years or emotionally neglects her, he has broken his vows even if he never divorces her. I (Ron) have said to many a self-righteous Christian man, "You didn't vow before God to abuse, manipulate, and use your wife; you vowed to love, honor, and cherish her. And since you stubbornly refuse to do so, what right do you have to blame your wife for emotionally shutting down or withdrawing from you sexually?" It is amazing how we can point fingers of blame to let ourselves off the hook.

If you are married to this man, enduring his distorted view of love is not a God-honoring marriage. He offers you a selfish love that is unwilling to learn. Bible scholar Kay Arthur explains true love like this: "Love—the agape kind that desires another's highest good—doesn't whitewash sin or allow wrong behavior to continue without confrontation. . . . A healthy relationship is one that is open. Things aren't buried, covered up, ignored, or denied, because when they are, decay sets in—putrefaction."[1] Insist on God's definition of love.

Leslie Vernick, author of *The Emotionally Destructive Relationship,* points out that biblical love doesn't just offer what the other person thinks they need; it loves them the way they really need to be loved. Accommodating a spouse's unhealthy relationship rules keeps both people stuck and isn't love. For example, subjecting yourself to your stepchildren's negative remarks while your husband idly stands by is not love. Communicating that you don't appreciate being treated that way and insisting that the children treat you with basic courtesy is loving.

If the situation doesn't change despite your repeated attempts, you may have to make strong statements and take firm action for the long-term good. You might say to your husband:

"I love you very much. And I long for a time when we both feel that the other is living up to our vows to love, honor, and

cherish. But I have to be honest with you. I don't feel that you cherish me 'above all others.' In fact, you should know by now that I feel completely defeated and pushed aside when you allow your children to speak to me disrespectfully. We've talked about this many times, yet you don't seem to hear me. Understand that I have too much respect for myself to let you or your children treat me this way.

"I have decided that when your children come to visit I will find another place to be and other things to do. I won't sit here and let them treat me that way. I'm not saying I won't ever be with your children; that's not realistic. But I don't have to subject myself to hours on end of their disrespect. I hope you enjoy your time with them this weekend.

"You also know that I haven't been interested in sex much lately. I have been closing myself off from you emotionally because of the hurtful words you say to me. My mind and body shut down, and I can't be free to give myself to you when you refuse to treat me decently. Please understand, this is not punishment or manipulation. Because I don't feel safe or cherished I just can't open myself to you emotionally and sexually. I'm not saying I won't ever have sex with you again. I long to have intimacy with you. But don't expect me to freely make love to you. Our relationship has to change for that to happen.

"I love you and will continue to pray for a more mutually satisfying marriage. What I won't do is accommodate your convenient definition of love. I want a marriage that seeks to love, honor, and cherish each other. I don't feel that from you and until you change, I will not subject myself to hurtful situations anymore."

Seek Help.

One of the best decisions I made was to see a counselor who understands stepfamilies. She has helped me to deal with the issues, and she also provided healthy self-examination.

Tara

Some of what you are coping with isn't fair, and you didn't bring it on yourself. But you do have to deal with it. If problems persist despite your efforts to change your circumstances, it's time to seek professional help. There are many things you can learn that will help your family through a challenging season of life. It's best if your husband attends with you, but if he won't, attend by yourself.

As prevalent as stepfamilies are in the world today, you'd think finding a therapist trained in stepfamily complications would be easy. It isn't. That's why Successful Stepfamilies, the ministry founded by Ron, offers phone coaching, counseling, and marriage intensive therapy for couples in crisis. For further information, visit *www. SuccessfulStepfamilies.com* and click on the Personal Help link.

Another option is to join or start a support group for stepmoms or stepfamily couples. Many of the local stepfamily ministries in America were started by someone like you. For example, get together with others and study this book. More resources are also available through Successful Stepfamilies. Find other stepmoms who need a friend. You don't have to struggle through this alone.

PRAYER

Dear Lord,

I'm embarrassed to admit it, but I feel like giving up and running away from home. Being a stepmom is much more complicated than I realized it would be, and it never seems to end. Thank you for comforting me when I'm afraid. I know that you see my pain because your Word says that you count my tears and you store them. They are precious to you. Just knowing that you care helps me to endure my situation. You still love me; you never leave. You keep your vows and promises to me. And I am grateful.

Lord, what I need is your strength and a new attitude. You say that you will take my hard heart and make it into one that's soft and loving. And you say you will put your spirit inside of me to provide wisdom and truth. I desperately long for your guidance—your ways. I often feel so overwhelmed and discouraged that I can't find a solution. That's when I feel like escaping.

Help me to discern when it's wise and right for me to speak up about what is wrong in my home, and when to keep silent. And guide me on how to handle these difficult circumstances. Give my husband eyes and a heart to see and understand the situation clearly. Teach him how to stand beside me and still love his kids.

You alone have the insight, compassion, and wisdom to show me how to "sing a new song." I look to you as my all in all. Thank you for loving me, even when I feel all alone.

PRAYER REFERENCES

Psalm 56:8; 73:22–23 *Ezekiel 36:24–27*
Deuteronomy 4:31 *Matthew 18:15*
Nehemiah 9:31–32 *Psalm 96:1–4*

Smart Stepmom Discussion Questions

1. When are the times that you feel like a stranger in your own home?

2. When are the times that you feel safe at home, and what's happening when you don't?

3. What do you sometimes dread about coming home?

4. How would you encourage a stepmom who feels like a "nobody" in her home?

5. Review the strategies in this chapter. Share any successes you may have had with them so others in your group can learn from your victories:

   • Change the Nest
   • Encourage Dad to Have Alone Time With His Kids
   • Girlfriends and More Girlfriends
   • Take Baby Steps
   • Start New Traditions

6. Those of you in extremely difficult situations could probably identify with the Manage Your Emotions and Fears section. Take the time to pray about your circumstances with your group. Do you need to seek help from a therapist or ministry leader?

7. If you are dealing with a spouse who refuses to discuss these issues, what new ways might you communicate your concerns?

Chapter 3

The Wicked Stepmother: Did Disney Have Me in Mind?

Wiping my own kids' snot is one thing. But wiping the snot of someone else's child is another.
An honest stepmom

I (Laura) know a man who formerly worked in the Imagineering Department at Disney World. One day during a brainstorming session he presented the idea that in addition to the lovely princesses, Disney should create figurines and toys based on the wicked women in the stories. He loved to hate the fiendish ladies, and he believed consumers did too. His superiors scoffed at the idea, claiming no one would buy such a toy. Who would want the wicked stepmother as a plaything? Ha! That was years ago. We now see Cinderella's evil stepmom everywhere, and you can probably find that black-and-white fur donned by Cruella de Vil at Neiman Marcus.

I wish I could brag that I've never been a wicked stepmother, but I have. I've wanted to pack my bags and join the—I was going to say circus but that's a lie, the smell is atrocious—maybe the Peace

Corps. Now and then don't you just want to run away, or lash out and say what you really feel, or dare I say it—be wicked?

There's a reason stepmoms get to this point. While you may be married to the best husband in the world, the complications of a stepfamily can bring out the worst—even in a godly, determined stepmom. There are a number of reasons for this. One of the most common is high expectations for your marriage, resulting in disappointment and disillusionment, giving you a sense of powerlessness and uncertainty. Listen to this stepmom's honest response to a Web forum as she shares her insights with a never-married woman who is engaged to a man with children.

> To the woman who is about to marry:
> I had thoughts of backing out before I said my vows; he had kids and I didn't. I had fears, but I read plenty of books and articles that minimized the issues I would face. They inspired me to move forward. I would give anything to be at that point in my life again. I wouldn't marry into this situation again for anything.
>
> I'm five years into the marriage and I still deeply love my husband, but I have faced so many challenges, disappointments, resentments, and regrets. The sacrifice is huge. I gave up the chance of having only my own family. I live in a home that does not feel like my own, and nasty thoughts that focus on his ex-wife or the money we have to give her every month come into my mind at the oddest times.
>
> Consider this: You will never have your husband's first-born child, and even in the rare situation where his kids like or even love you, you may always wonder what it would have been like if you only had your own children. I view marriage as sacred and never want to be divorced. This and my faith are the only reasons I am still married today. But I wish someone would have told it to me straight. Don't ignore your inner voice. Meticulously evaluate your decision to marry a man with kids. Much heartache can be avoided if you pick a different path for your life. Life as a stepmother is very lonely, draining, and almost never rewarding. Even if you don't have custody of the kids it's non-stop. If someone had told me what I'm telling you, I may not have believed it would be this bad, and I probably

would have married him anyway. But nobody really tried to tell me. There is a reason why second marriages fail more than first marriages.

These are the things I thought would heal over time because I was getting such a great husband. However, love does not change the fact that he has kids and a former wife.

I hope and pray that you will give what I've shared some consideration. Unlike many stepmoms, I have a good relationship with his former wife and both of his kids. My husband is very supportive, and his kids do not disrespect me. In the stepfamily world, I have it about as good as it gets. But this is the hardest and most heartbreaking thing I have ever experienced.

Those words are hard to hear, and some may feel they are too negative. But like the woman who wrote them, I (Laura) didn't understand how complicated and lonely my life as a stepmom would be. Because I was naïve I made many mistakes. In order to encourage you in your walk as a stepmother, this chapter exposes the things I did wrong, which often contributed to my "wickedness." If I had it to do over again, these are the things I would do differently. Years later I still work on many of these areas.

Someone once said, "Learn from the mistakes of others; you won't live long enough to make them all yourself." I hope you can learn from mine.

Accept the Things You Cannot Change

During our weekend visits with his kids I tried to change things, such as poor eating habits. Big mistake. It wasn't my job. The biological mom was fine with how they ate. It wasn't a "hill to die on," and the battle only created stress.

In addition, I needed to accept and understand that my in-laws were grieving for their grandchildren and the loss of the biological family. Their sorrow caused them to side with the kids during conflict, and they sabotaged what we were trying to accomplish.

Wisdom knows there are some things not worth blowing up over, like when they sneak the kids pizza and a soda after a turkey dinner they refused to eat. Use discernment when deciding what to confront.

I also had to accept that I could not force my stepkids to want God in their lives. The Holy Spirit has been capable of drawing people to his side for thousands of years; he does not need my help. My job is to remain close to the vine, Jesus Christ, and abide in him consistently. I hear from stepmoms who are so desperate to get the kids into church and convert them to Christianity that they end up pushing them further away. Yes, you want to influence your stepchildren toward Christ as much as you can, but ultimately it's Dad's job to give them firm guidance about Jesus and church. If he refuses, then it's his price to pay as he stands before God one day. In our home they see Christ as a day-to-day part of our life, and my job now is to pray diligently for them.

Another thing to accept is that you can't change the biological mom or her poor choices. She may talk about you behind your back to the kids, family members, friends, etc. Remain a lady. When you hear a lie, don't explode. Remain calm and respond with the truth. Here's an example of how one stepmom did this: "Joshua, I'm sorry your mom is telling you that I don't care about you and your sister. That must be very confusing and painful to hear. I want you to know that it's just not true. I care very much about you, and I want to get to know you even more. I know that being close to me will likely put you in an uncomfortable situation with your mom. I'm not trying to compete with your mother; you can allow me to love you and it won't take anything away from you and your mother. But I also know this might be hard to do and that stepfamilies can be complicated. If there is something specific I can do to ease the tension concerning your mom, just let me know. Would you like to help me make dinner, and we can talk about what happened in school today?"

Dig Into Your Past

One of the things I discovered in my second marriage was that I had unhealed wounds from my past that had nothing to do with the stepfamily. During some Christian counseling, my destructive enabling, rescuing, people-pleasing, and codependent (phrases that mean similar things) behavior was revealed.

I grew to understand how from childhood a person can become codependent, and that enabling looks and feels noble, but in reality it's selfish. It seems loving to prevent a loved one from suffering a consequence when they make a poor choice, but the root reason a codependent steps in to rescue another is the need to fill a hole in his or her own heart. It's an attempt to control others and to feel loved or significant. Often the root cause of codependency is the fear of being rejected or abandoned.

Are *you* a people pleaser? Here are some ways to tell. Do you:

- avoid conflict at all costs, believing that submission means "keeping the peace"?
- allow guilt to prevent you from saying no?
- have a sense of dread, fear, or anger if not in control of a situation?
- hear yourself saying, "It's not really that bad" or "I'm the reason he treats me that way"?
- fear retaliation or removal of love if you say no or set a self-care boundary to the point that you constantly cater to others?
- walk on eggshells even in your own home?
- ignore destructive circumstances that you know should be addressed?
- allow people to speak to you in a disrespectful manner?
- make excuses for rude and offensive behavior?
- isolate from others or fear what people think of you?

- refuse to discuss problems or seek help?
- take on the responsibility of someone who is negligent?
- try to control others by creating a feeling of superiority, and/or treat your spouse like a child?
- distort God's teaching about mercy, viewing leniency as an act of love, so that you tolerate sin?

Ouch! If you checked more than two or three you may be wincing. Don't be discouraged. If God taught me how to overcome the people-pleasing disease, he can do the same for you. Please research resources that address codependency, and get counseling. It's often difficult to overcome without help.

I also find that many stepmoms battle trying to control others around them. It's a desire to "rein in" other people in an attempt to stabilize the circumstances. Stepmoms often ask, "How can I get . . ."

- my husband to stand up to his kids?
- the biological mom to stop saying horrible things about me?
- my stepkids to respect me and appreciate all that I do for them?
- my in-laws to accept me?
- my husband to see my pain and loneliness and spend time alone with me?
- his kids to go to church?

My answer to them is always the same. "You can't." By your character you can influence others to be more accepting or respectful, but ultimately you can't control their behavior. You can't change another person, but you can make it more difficult for them to remain in destructive patterns.

It's often hard to overcome the temptation to control others.

To discover how, you may need to read a book on the subject (like *Boundaries* by Henry Cloud and John Townsend), attend a support group, or seek counseling.

Give Everyone Some Space

One of the biggest mistakes I made as a stepmom was not recognizing that his kids needed time alone with their dad. Now adults, they have shared with us that they felt like I came into their dad's life and overnight everything changed. They remember our getting married much more quickly than we actually did. My husband, Steve, should have maintained alone time with the boys during our courtship and after our marriage. But when I entered the picture their dad seemed to disappear, which caused them to resent me.

Allowing your spouse to maintain one-on-one time with his kids is vitally important. And it provides you with time alone that can be well spent either enjoying the peace and quiet or with your children, family, or girlfriends.

Watch Your Tongue

Sometimes I'm negative about my stepsons and the decisions they make. This creates a wall between my husband and me because they are his children, and to him it feels as though I am being critical. It has taken a lot of time and much prayer, but I try to seek God's guidance as to what, when, and how to mention a subject. If I ask myself, "Is it necessary to mention this?" then I can usually determine if I should share it or not.

Other stepmoms are guilty of aggressive and harsh judgment of their husband's parenting or children. Comments like "your brat kid" or (regarding an adult stepchild) "your son can't make good decisions" invite defensiveness from your husband, which polarizes the two of you against each other. You'll blame him for siding with his children and not hearing you, and he'll accuse you of being mean and exaggerating things. You'll both end up feeling resentful and lonely.

Also dangerous is contemptuous name-calling or negative critiques of your husband's previous life choices and extended family. One woman continually referred to her husband's ex-wife as his "trailer trash." Another called her in-laws and husband's siblings "crazy control freaks." Such mean-spirited judgments push your husband away. As Paul admonishes, use words to build others up (Ephesians 4:29); otherwise, if you can't say something nice, don't say anything at all.

Understand That Holidays and Vacations Will Be Different

I finally learned that I'll always be on the "outside." Holidays and vacations make it even more obvious (which is why we have an entire chapter addressing special family days later in the book). We are not a biological family; there are different dynamics at play.

I'm not one of those women who *goos* and *gaas* over babies in the mall, and I have no regret over not having any biological children. But even I struggle to some degree on Mother's Day. I think my husband feels worse for me on that day than I do, and that helps! I usually get a nice brunch out of it, which we enjoy together. But the reason many stepmoms struggle with Mother's Day is because it's a stark reminder of the numerous sacrifices you have made with your heart, husband, time, money, and hard work while receiving little in return.

I don't want my stepsons to fawn over me on Mother's Day; they have a mom and I'm not her. Now that they have wives and their own kids, they sometimes like to celebrate together, and that's great. The best Mother's Day present I ever got was from my stepson Todd several years ago. Billy Graham's new autobiography was hot off the press, and Todd got a copy right away. He knows faith is important to me, and he proudly drove during the night to bring me the new release. It's my fondest Mother's Day memory because he took the time to do something special for me.

Special moments like this come from time to time, but when you feel like an outsider, find a way to soothe your hurt. Remind yourself that your family is not done cooking yet.

Your Affections Will Differ

For years I felt guilty that I didn't love his kids the same way I do my nieces and nephew, who are like my own children. It wasn't until I read information explaining this was normal that I began to understand and accept the emotions. I love my stepfamily, which now includes daughters-in-law and grandchildren. I just love them differently than I do my own biological family.

One stepmom called this the absence of "mom-like" feelings for the children. Some guilt for feeling this way is understandable; you have high expectations for yourself and want your husband to be pleased with how you love his children. However, don't be excessive in your guilt; it only makes you anxious and needy. Love chosen is still love.

Finances Will Be Difficult

When you marry a man with kids you must accept that the money is going to be tight. He is commanded by God to support those children and provide for their needs (not always their wants) (1 Timothy 5:8). However, when I felt my hard-earned money was being wasted or used foolishly, I was resentful. I had to surrender all of that and let my husband take care of it (he is trustworthy). How his former wife used the child support was not my battle. When the kids needed something specific (such as braces), we tried to pay that directly to the professional whenever possible. This helped to ease the tension.

Discipline and the Kids

We spend a great deal of time on this subject in other chapters, so I'll just briefly share that I had to put aside the way I was raised and how my mom disciplined me growing up. When I expected his kids to behave or respond as I did when I was a child, I set myself up for failure and frustration.

It is a misstep to insist on a rigid structure in the home that differs from what the children are used to. You may have been raised to make your bed each morning and pick up your room before breakfast, but if they have not, do not instantly try to raise the standard. The wider the gap between your expectations and your husband's (and what the children are accustomed to), the more patient you must be about change.

Remember Their Pain

One of the things I suggest to stepmoms over and over again is to volunteer at a divorce-recovery-for-kids program. This will give you much needed insight into the mind, heart, and life of the child of divorce. I was a child of divorce, and it's horrible. It changed my life. If the kids don't get the help they need, the pain can ferment and affect other relationships. Therefore, I highly suggest reading books and attending a support group.

This can also provide topics for conversation and possibly much-needed alone time with the stepkids. Share what you are learning in the support group. This will reveal that you are trying to understand their pain. Remember that hurt people—hurt people.

Little Things Do Mean a Lot

One of the things I didn't do as much in my early years as a stepmom, but that I try to do more now, is to notice the things that mean a lot to my stepkids and their families—especially the grandkids. I don't do them to receive a response but merely as a way to show them I care and that I desire to continue building the relationship.

For example, my stepson Scott loves cars. I heard my step-daughter-in-law mention that he would like a model of a certain old Chevelle. Periodically, I would try to find the one he wanted, but had no success. During a speaking engagement I flew out of the Detroit airport, where I noticed a store filled with model cars. They had the one Scott wanted. It was heavy and my bag didn't have much room, but I was determined to get that gift on the plane with me.

We gave him the car for Christmas, and I'm sure he liked it. But it was my husband who knew how difficult it had been to find and how I had searched to find something that his son wanted. It's those little things that communicate "I care" that sometimes mean a lot.

God Can Teach You to Love

Loving people who don't seem to like you isn't an easy task. It takes supernatural power. I continuously pray for God to show me how to love and show kindness to my stepfamily and the biological mom.

One of the things I share with those who are divorcing, and that I wish I had done with my stepsons, is to take the child and buy a small gift for the biological mom for a special occasion such as her birthday. This communicates to the child that it's all right to love both parents. And as a stepmom it communicates that you understand the child is being placed in the middle. It can ease the child's tension. I know . . . I know. I can hear the weeping and gnashing of teeth already. This is Jesus-like love to the max!

Keep the Commitment

I'd be lying if I didn't admit that sometimes the only reason I remained married was because I made a vow before God to stay "for better or worse." I made a commitment to do my part to make the marriage healthy and whole. Sometimes that means keeping my mouth shut, sometimes that means praying, sometimes that means allowing my husband or the kids to suffer a consequence, sometimes it means learning how to love the unlovable. But in every circumstance I have God's promise that he will never leave me, and that he will continuously renew my mind with his mind. It's a promise (see Romans 12:1–2; Philippians 2:1–11).

When I become weary and feel like giving up, I take the wounds, rejections, and frustrations to the only One who truly understands my pain—Jesus. He fully comprehends what it's like to pour yourself into people who make fun of, scoff at, snub, and ridicule you. Although my husband should support and love me, he can't heal me. It is not his job to mend my wounds.

PRAYER

Heavenly Daddy,

I confess! I'm wicked—and sometimes I like it. Even though I detest the phrase "wicked stepmother," if I'm being totally honest, there are days when I feel as if it describes me perfectly. I want to hurt those who are hurting me. I want to retaliate even though I know it's childish, foolish, ungodly, and unproductive. Help!

I need to understand why it seems like nasty thoughts and actions are the only way to protect myself. I know there is a more constructive way to respond to my husband and his kids. I need your advice. I need a better way to live.

If my past is still dictating my future or my behavior, show me, Lord. I want that cleansed out of my inner being. When I'm stuck in a destructive cycle of people pleasing, or if I try to control others, teach me how to stop.

Thank you for showing me that it's not unnatural for me to love my own biological children or extended family more than I do my stepkids. But I also ask that you would increase my love for my step-kids, Lord. And help me to see them as you see them. Guide my mind to understand how they think and where they ache or struggle so that I can know the best ways to help them.

The bottom line is I'm lost without you. And there will never be enough words to say thank you for loving me and providing me with an abundant life. I praise you that I can be filled with your hope, promises, love, and security. Amen.

PRAYER REFERENCES

Psalm 86	*2 Chronicles 30:9*
Exodus 33:19	*John 10:10*

Smart Stepmom Discussion Questions

1. Does the phrase "wicked stepmother" bother you? Why or why not?

2. Why do you think some stepmoms feel or act wicked?

3. How do you respond to the comments from the stepmom who shares her experience with the engaged woman? If you were talking to a woman who is engaged to a man with children, what advice would you share with her?

4. What are some of the issues you would like to learn how to accept as a normal part of stepfamily living? How can you take steps in that direction?

5. Are there concerns from your past that still affect your life? Have you swept under the rug issues associated with:

   • Dysfunction in your childhood
   • Former relationships or divorce
   • Molestation, rape, or violence
   • Abortion
   • Self-loathing
   • Drug or alcohol abuse in your home

6. What's the hardest part of controlling your tongue? Are there practical steps that might make it easier?

7. Does it make you feel better to know that feeling like an outsider is a normal emotion for many stepmoms?

8. Are you surprised to learn that it's understandable to love your own children more than you do your stepkids? Does this help with any guilt you may have experienced?

9. Are you willing to volunteer at a divorce recovery support group for kids to help you to understand your stepchildren's pain? Is your husband willing?

10. What are one or two ways you can do a "little thing" for your stepkids that might show them you are trying to build a bridge? Be prepared that they might not show any appreciation for your kind gestures for several years.

Chapter 4

Understanding His Kids (Part 1): Loss, Grief, and Troubling Emotions

I never saw it coming but I felt it and heard it every day, Mom cursing at Dad and my dad yelling back. I yelled at both of them to stop but it made no difference . . . things are different and the house has crumbled and I couldn't stop it.
          Chaz R., age 7
          From a school assignment
          he entitled "The House Crumbles"

Today as I (Ron) write this it's September 11, the anniversary of one of the most horrific days in United States history, and national TV is replaying broadcasts of the fateful day. Reliving the tragedy, I watch terrifying scenes of hijacked planes crashing into buildings and brave heroes running to their death in an attempt to save others. As the images transport me back to that evil day, I see massive buildings crumble, and lost, crying children wandering the streets as they look for parents. It was a nation in chaos, panic, and shock.

Like most Americans, I remember exactly where I was when

the 9/11 attacks occurred. The trauma of that day is seared into our memories; we cannot escape it. We felt secure before 2001, but the terrorists violated that confidence. The United States changed that day—forever.

When tragedy penetrates our life, it leaves unforgettable marks on our soul and psyche. Shortly after 9/11/2001 an out-of-control airplane was spotted in the New York airspace. In an understandable post-traumatic reaction, numerous people were overcome with fear. They wondered if danger was approaching once again. Before the 9/11 attacks most would have watched with concern and viewed it as a benign, unfortunate event for those onboard. But after 9/11, benign events became a possible malignancy *for everyone.*

Your husband's children have experienced their own 9/11. The death of their mother or the death of the family to divorce caused a severe trauma that has left a residue of grief and pain. In addition to losing the biological structure of the family, it's highly possible that your stepkids have suffered:

- the loss of security and control over their lives
- the shock that hope can be destroyed
- the realization that parents can lie and do hurtful things
- the insecurity that tomorrow is unpredictable
- the trauma that God may answer prayer in a way that disappoints us or causes sadness
- the realization that despite what the pastor says, marriage is not always forever.

Understand that your stepchild's world has crumbled with the same ferocity as the collapse of the twin towers.

Losses of this magnitude can forever alter a child's perspective on life. Like it or not, loss is a living part of the child and it *must not* be minimized. When you decided to become a stepmom, you assumed the role of helping grieving children. This will require patience and a commitment to understanding the impact and damage that has occurred. Acknowledging how deeply your stepkids have been affected, both during and after their crisis, will prepare you to love and nurture them as they cope.

THE ENDURING NATURE OF LOSS

Be merciful to me, O Lord, for I am in distress;
my eyes grow weak with sorrow,
my soul and my body with grief.
                                        Psalm 31:9

If you live long enough, you'll probably experience some form of loss. However, most people don't understand the toll bereavement takes on us. Familiar models of grief suggest that loss is a linear experience. Elizabeth Kubler-Ross in her book *On Death and Dying* suggests that grieving people move through the stages of shock and denial in a linear fashion. They start with anger, then move on to bargaining, depression, and finally to acceptance. While this does articulate the experience of many adults (each experience is unique), it does not adequately describe the experience of children. Their grief has distinctive qualities that many adults, including stepmoms, don't realize. Let's explore the enduring nature of grief for children.

What do you believe occurs for the person who reaches the acceptance stage? Does "getting over it" mean they have moved past the grief so it doesn't debilitate them any longer? In our "check it off the list and move on" society we falsely assume that acceptance means the loss no longer impacts our life. This simply isn't true. Acceptance essentially means that a person comes to terms with the reality of their loss and chooses to live in spite of it. The sorrow still lingers, but the intensity is lessened. When a person chooses to process the grief they still have questions, but they aren't emotionally

A Quick Turnaround

Whether following the death of a parent or a divorce, adolescents and older children can form resentment when a parent quickly begins to date. For the child, a new relationship betrays the family, and it discounts their sadness. It's important to remember that children are at least one year behind their parent in the grieving process. We recommend that biological parents wait at least two years after the death of a spouse or a divorce before dating. This will help to prevent short-circuiting the child's grief process, which can form a wedge of resentment toward your marriage. A long-term engagement is advised as well.

paralyzed anymore. The consequences of the loss are still unwelcome but can be faced head on.

Over time, children may reach some measure of acceptance of the loss of their biological family. But the child's pervasive fantasy is for things to return as they were before. After parental divorce when teens or young adults are asked, "Should your parents be together?" they often reply, "No way. They just can't be together; it's best that they divorced." However, when asked, "If you were God for the day and you could orchestrate your family any way you wanted it, what would you do?" they almost unanimously place Mom and Dad back together. Even children with a deceased parent desire for him or her to be resurrected and the family reunited.

The bottom line is that loss changes children. They do not completely "get over it" and become the innocent, happy little adults we wish they were. Loss leaves children in a state of ambiguity; they cope with what remains all the while longing for what they wish could happen. This doesn't eliminate the possibility of establishing a loving relationship with your stepchildren, but it will complicate it.

Developmental Grieving

The manner in which children process grief is one example of how bereavement is different for children than for adults. With each developmental stage of growth and during major life transitions, a child will grieve their losses again and again. Developmental stages include cognitive, emotional, and relational transitions. This includes, for example, the onset of puberty, when a child's body begins to mature into a man or woman and their mind shifts from concrete, black-and-white thinking to more abstract, logical thinking. During this stage of brain development a child's ability to see the other side of issues and events increases, thereby allowing the boy or girl to consider a new point of view. For example, the son who was too young to remember his parents' divorce begins to imagine what caused the breakup. Unfortunately, along with imagination comes heartache.

A child who had believed Dad's explanation for the divorce, for example, may begin to question his words. Years after the divorce these new insights into "what really happened" can evoke angry emotions toward Dad—and perhaps toward you.

A relational developmental transition occurs when a young teenager has his or her first romantic relationship. The excitement of a first kiss followed by the pain of a breakup may lead the child to grieve their parents' divorce all over again. For the first time the child understands the rejection that one parent may have felt when abandoned by the other.

Developmental grieving often catches stepmoms (and dads) off guard. Yesterday they seemed fine, today they are hurt and angry. What changed? Any number of life experiences and internal developmental changes can stimulate and resurface the grief. A huge mistake parents often make is to assume that because they have moved on, the children have too. Another common misconception is when widowers assume their

Befriending Adult Stepchildren

Without question adult stepchildren are impacted by loss too. They will carry childhood losses into adulthood or, if experienced in adulthood, will grieve them over time.

Whereas developmental stages are triggers for grief in children, life transitions are for adults. Don't be surprised if a wedding, birth of a grandchild, graduation, or extended-family death causes grief to again ripple to the surface. Take a step back when this occurs and give them time to find their way through the sadness.

children will do fine with a stepmom because it wasn't a divorce that severed the family. In either case, grief remains.

Life transitions may arouse a new layer of grief. For example, high school graduation is supposed to be a time of celebration. But for the child whose parents can't be in the same room with each other—even during a party—graduation can trigger more sadness and suffering. As the child observes friends from intact families having a day of enjoyment, this child experiences resentment, sorrow, and possibly anger. I (Laura) painfully remember my high school graduation, when the school didn't provide enough reserved seating for both sides of my family. What should have been a happy day in my life turned into one more stressful, nauseating battle. No matter what decision I made for the "exclusive" seats, someone was going to be mad at me. And it wasn't because anyone in my family was overly concerned about where they sat; it was one more "control war" to see who would win.

A wedding is another life transition that rekindles sadness. Deciding who will walk her down the aisle can be an excruciating decision for a young bride. Or the daughter who has just delivered her firstborn may be wondering if her mom and stepmom are fighting in the hospital waiting room. For the child of divorce, each of these events can trigger the loss of what "should have been." Years have come and gone, but grief—and rage—can be ignited.

A Cumulative Impact

The consequences of loss are cumulative. Mom dying is difficult enough, but don't forget to add the pain of moving to a new home because of financial changes. This transition might bring a loss of neighborhood friends, a change in school (that perhaps years later still doesn't feel safe), the feeling of being treated differently by people at church, and a physical distance from Mom's family. The accumulation of loss goes on and on. A daughter who before Mom's death enjoyed being her "kitchen apprentice" now makes dinner on her own three nights a week. The son who once received hugs before bedtime now feels empty and lonely because Dad is spread thin.

Recognize this significant fact: There is probably no one in your home who has experienced more loss than your stepchildren or your own kids from a previous marriage. Further, realize that your marriage was another loss for your stepchildren. It was a gain for you and your husband, but a loss for the children. Your marriage may eventually bring great benefit to the kids (which may or may not be appreciated for some time), but it also brought loss and changes they didn't ask for. This doesn't mean you should get a divorce or feel guilty, but you should offer compassion for the cumulative impact.

The accumulation of loss is why there may be strong negative reactions when small changes occur. When a child's reaction doesn't fit the circumstances, you may be witnessing the cumulative effects of loss. For example, everyone is sad when a boyfriend or girlfriend breaks up with him or her. But a child who dives into depression or panic after a breakup—and stays there—is probably overloaded with accumulated grief. Showing compassion is vital, but refrain from letting your mercy or guilt paralyze your response as a parent mentor. If a child's behavior requires a consequence, you and your husband must find a way to discipline as well as "hug their hurt." It's the combination of compassion and setting limits that helps children grieve while learning to respect boundaries.

When Connie's fifteen-year-old stepson, Kyle, went through a terrible breakup with his girlfriend, she tried to be compassionate and talk with him. But Kyle abruptly shut her out and made some hurtful comments toward Connie. This Smart Stepmom struck a balance in her response: "I'm really sorry about the situation with your girlfriend; I can see you are hurting. But I don't deserve to be spoken to in that manner. It's okay to be hurt and frustrated, but that doesn't give you the right to be disrespectful toward me. If you continue to talk to me in that way, your dad and I will implement a consequence."

Unequal Losses

Not all loss is equal. Christian author and noted grief therapist H. Norman Wright shares that the nature and circumstances surrounding a loss alter the course of the grief process.[1] The more complicated the circumstances, the more prolonged and complicated grieving becomes. For example, the loss over a parent with a terminal illness begins long before the actual death. The unexpected loss of a mother or father killed in a car wreck may extend grieving for many years. In addition, when grief is accompanied by extreme negative circumstances (such as homicide), bereavement is even more prolonged and complicated. Finally, a parent's suicide often produces several years of active grief before the intensity of sadness decreases; even then resolution is not found unless the nature of the death is openly explored with other family members.

Similarly, a parental divorce that happens quickly due to an affair affects the kids differently than one in which the couple has been arguing and threatening divorce in front of the kids for years. The children are still deeply affected, but grief will follow a different course. Researchers have discovered that the negative impact of divorce on children is worse when the parents' marriage had low conflict, as opposed to those with high conflict levels. The former brings an unexpected and uncontrollable loss, leaving the children to wrestle with the shame of parents who didn't seem to try hard enough.[2]

It's unwise to predict the length of time your stepchildren will require to recover from their losses. Further, refrain from equating your losses with those of your stepchild. Smart Stepmoms take time to ponder the unique issues their stepkids experience over many years and remain open to how grief will manifest itself.

Resurrected Grief and Walls of Self-Protection

When you consider all that we have described, it's easier to understand why and how a child's grief can be resurrected. Grief is not merely a thing of the past, but also the present. Confusion, anger, depression, sadness, and irritability can be triggered by seemingly benign occurrences.

Loss triggers a constant fear of more loss. Before experiencing loss, both children and adults assume that life is predictable and safe. I (Laura) lived a large portion of my life looking over my shoulder, wondering when the next catastrophe would hit. I was in my forties when I discovered that I felt responsible for my parents' divorce. That unfounded burden carried with it tremendous shame and guilt, which dictated my behavior from eight years of age until adulthood. Loss teaches us that life is not safe. Bad things *can* happen. When I became a Christian at twenty-four, Jesus saved my soul, but he didn't erase all of my memories or distorted thinking. With God's guidance I eventually received the professional help I needed to fully recover. It's been a long process, but I'm finally free.

Children (and adults) can erect walls of self-protection designed to keep out more hurt. This might explain the hot/cold responses you may receive from your stepchildren. One minute they are warm and friendly and appreciative, the next they are cold and distant. Keeping a stepmom at arm's length guards against hurt (and manages loyalty conflicts). Loving you is a complicated task for the child. So what can you do?

- *Be patient and allow the children to set the pace for the relationship.* Give them the freedom to vacillate between a close and distant relationship with you, while still showing respect. Physical affection from the kids may vary from moment to moment (or weekend to weekend). For example, if they call you Mom, great. If that changes to your first name after a weekend at the biological mom's house, don't worry. It's merely grief in motion, not personal rejection.

- *Refrain from allowing how they treat you to dictate how you respond.* Give the gift of your consistent, unconditional grace. Prove yourself to be a safe person.

- *Move very slowly with issues of discipline and punishment.* Quickly forcing yourself on them as a parent will backfire. Instead become one of the many parental figures in their life (e.g., teachers, coaches, youth pastors). Forcing your way into their life won't work. (We'll share more on this subject in chapters 7 and 8.)

- *Don't try to be Wonder Woman.* You are conscientious and desire to serve your family well, but accept the stepfamily dynamics that you can't control. If you can't win the kids over immediately, don't berate yourself. The Crockpot is still cooking.

- *Learn to appreciate and enjoy today.* Obsessing over the dream of permanent inclusion in a child's heart causes you to live in tomorrow rather than fully enjoying today. If you have a solid relationship, ride the occasional waves of sadness with them and don't take it personally.

DR. STEPMOM: GRIEF COUNSELOR

We believe that both you and your husband can help the children with their enduring grief. Think of yourself as a grief counselor. To be effective, a few essential skills will be required.

Practice Emotional Coaching

Permitting sadness and (appropriate) expressions of grief is the foundation for grief counseling. You cannot fix the child's pain, but you can hug it. A small child who falls and skins their knee will most assuredly cry out in pain. Putting medicine and a Band-Aid on the abrasion helps, but affection is what really matters. Holding and consoling the child helps the hurt. It doesn't fix the skinned knee, but the child feels better. In similar fashion you can help your stepchild with the wounds to his or her heart. Allow them to cry over what hurts. Knowing you care is what makes a difference.

One compassionate way to respond in those moments is with emotional coaching. Most children (and adults) are driven by their emotions and don't know how to manage them. Scripture makes it clear that we are to be transformed by the renewing of our minds (Romans 12:2); putting our Spirit-led mind in charge of our emotions is a skill for every disciple. It also helps children manage their grief.

> ### Smart Dating
>
> You may not have realized until now how much a child's past is forced into your lap when you marry their father. Better to discover this now than be blindsided by it later.
>
> Give prayerful consideration to your readiness to take on this emotional weight. The child's grief is not yours to resolve, but you will have to minister to it, and it will impact your place in the home. Move forward with eyes wide open.

Grief is an emotion that demands center stage; it cannot be denied. In his excellent book *Raising an Emotionally Intelligent Child*, Dr. John Gottman states that parents should teach children to recognize how their emotions are impacting them and how to self-regulate their behavior in spite of their emotions. He outlines a number of steps to emotion coaching. Begin by being aware of your own emotions and what you are feeling in the moment. Managing yourself appropriately models what you are teaching the child to do.

Next, seek out the key emotions in what the child is saying and label them. Small children, for example, frequently don't have the vocabulary to label their emotions. Further, they act mad, not recognizing that sadness lies beneath. Reveal this to them as a way to help connect the experience with the emotion. "I can tell you are really angry and perhaps a little sad right now. Do you know what you are sad about?" This is important because it centers the conversation on the heart. A child may be upset about a present circumstance (e.g., an unforeseen change in schedule), but focusing solely on that won't help them deal with the more enduring hurt that is connected to the past.

Remember grief is a journey, not a destination. Therefore after labeling the emotion, fight the temptation to fix it. At funerals we often hear misguided attempts to temper emotional pain. "Don't feel bad. God needed another angel." "I'm sorry for your loss. I'm sure you'll feel better when you realize that they're in a better place." These are sorry attempts to heal sorrow, and they don't work. These comments minimize pain and make the person feel isolated in their grief. What causes us to make these comments? When people are hurting it makes us uncomfortable, so we attempt to alleviate their pain . . . and ours. Learning how to hear and endure your stepchild's sadness is a key element to helping them walk through it.

Finally, while labeling the child's emotion is a good first step, getting to the root cause should bring added relief. Consider this example of a child who returns home after a weekend at Mom's house. Ten-year-old Brennan walks in the door snippy and curt. Not his usual self, Brennan speaks to his stepmom, Carmen, in a disrespectful tone. In the past Carmen has interpreted such behavior as rejection, which activates her fear that she will never be considered an "insider" in the home. She would snap back at Brennan and the two would fuss at each other until she sent him to his room to wait for his father's return home. This time, she calmed her fears and focused in on Brennan's experience.

Brennan: [in a harsh, disrespectful tone] "Do I still have to do my chores tonight? I already did some at my mom's house. It's not fair!" [Stepparents make easy targets for the frustrations children feel; try to remember that much of what is directed at you is not about you.]

Part-Time Stepmoms

Time contributes to a child's trust. Having a limited amount of time with children may slow your "cooking" speed with them. Without the trust that comes from a deepening relationship, a child may not be willing to share their grief with you. You may be able to label their emotions, for example, but not get them to talk openly about them. Do what you can to show yourself as someone they can trust and see if, over time, they open their heart to you.

Carmen: [She momentarily sidesteps the disrespect and in a calming tone begins to label the emotions she hears.] "Hold on a second. I can tell you are really irritated about having to do chores twice. Am I getting that right?"

Brennan: "Yes. Your son only has to do chores in one house, and I have to do them at my mom's house and here. It's not fair." [This response baits Carmen to take the issue personally.]

Carmen: [She dodges the bait and stays centered on Brennan's emotion, wondering what's behind it.] "You're feeling put upon because you have to do chores twice. I can see how you might feel that way. [That last part disarms Brennan a little.] I'm also wondering if you are angry you had to leave your mom's house and come here. It's hard to do that, isn't it?"

Brennan: [now refocused on what is beneath the chores issue] "I guess so."

Carmen: [digs a little deeper] "Does it hurt when you enjoy being with your mom and then have to leave? I can see why you might come home a little grumpy and sad."

Brennan: [calming down] "It's not fair that I have to leave; I only get three days there and Mom cries when I leave. I hate that."

Carmen: [Realizing how deep his sadness is, she replies with soft compassion.] "I'm sorry, Brennan. That really stinks for you. I know your mom loves you very much, and we love you too. This situation must cause you to feel divided in trying to love us back, and I'll bet that's very hard on you." [There's no attempt to fix his emotions, just acknowledgment. Carmen now notices that the tone of the conversation is softening because the emotion is shifting away from anger to sadness; Carmen is helping Brennan connect to what really bothers him. She now "wonders" about other emotions he might be feeling . . .] "You feel sad about leaving your mom—and you should. It's hard leaving her. I'm wondering when you see her crying if you also feel guilty for leaving her?"

Brennan: "Sort of."

Carmen: "I regret that for you. I can see how you might feel that way, but please know that none of this is your fault. Because your parents divorced, you don't have any choice but to go back and forth between them. I really am sorry you get caught in the middle. Could I give you a hug—or do you need a little more time first?" [TLC at its best. She gives him a verbal hug just by saying she wants to hug him and permission not to physically hug her if he can't do so comfortably right now.]

Brennan: [showing how torn he is] "I'm not quite ready yet."

Carmen: "Okay. I'll hug you later when it feels okay for you." [At this point Carmen has earned the right to address the initial disrespect that started the conversation. Carmen can now balance her compassion with setting limits.] "You know, a little while ago you spoke harshly to me. I know you came home feeling cruddy, but I don't deserve to be spoken to that way. I don't appreciate it and don't want you to do it again. Next time, if you come home feeling yucky, I'd rather you walk in and tell me that so I know to give you some space until you feel better. That way we won't get fussy with each other. Could you do that?" [Pause] "I would appreciate an apology." [Waits for response.] "I'm still going to give you that hug later. You can go now."

I (Ron) have counseled many people who at this point say, "Yeah, right. There's no way this child is going to start identifying his emotions or controlling his actions." My typical response is, "How do you know? You've never empowered your child or stepchild with emotional coaching before. You don't know what they are capable of. Try it and see." Time and again these doubters become believers.

If compassion and understanding aren't enough to help a child begin to control themselves when they are sad, you and your husband will need to impose a consequence for his behavior. Either way, the emotional coaching should continue because over time it creates a bridge of connection and trust.

Emotional coaching is not something you try once and then everything gets better. Depending on how old a child or young adult is, and how much anger is bottled up inside, you may have to work tirelessly for a long time before you see changes, but start now. You have nothing to lose and a child to gain.

A LONG-TERM PERSPECTIVE

A few years ago a woman named Heather attended my (Ron's) conference for stepfamilies. She was dating a man with three children and considering becoming a stepmom. After the conference she wrote me a thank-you note and shared her perspectives. As an adult child of divorce, Heather had experienced multiple losses in her life. Her parents had remarried, so she also knew what it was like to have a stepparent. These experiences gave her an uncharacteristic wisdom and insight into stepparenting children after loss. With her permission, we share her comments. Pay close attention to how she weaves her understanding of her own loss into her perspective on being a stepmom.

When Mom Is Deceased

Effective grieving of a deceased parent includes carrying the memory of that parent throughout life. This allows a child or adult to celebrate their heritage and cherish the special contributions of that parent to their life.

Utilize the natural triggers of life (e.g., eating at a parent's favorite restaurant) to ask questions about the parent. Be open to their stories and openly celebrate special memories with them.

• "Your mom sure was a good cook. It's obvious why everyone put her in charge of Thanksgiving dinner. I bet you miss that."

• "I came across a box the other day that contained cards people sent your mom while she was ill. Your dad and I thought you might like to have them. She must have been deeply loved by many friends."

Jim and I have been dating for two years; he has three teenagers and I adore them. It's easy for me to deal with potential stepchildren because I am one. I've been where they are, and as a result, I don't have the expectations that some stepparents have. I don't freak out if a kid doesn't hug me. It doesn't bother me that they talk about their mom, and it's okay that Jim has his "kid day" without me. I've been there. It's funny, if Jim's daughter doesn't hug me (like at Christmas), it really bothers him, but not me. I don't always hug my stepparents. In fact,

I almost never do—and not because I don't love them or like them—I just don't do it. There doesn't need to be a reason.

He talks about how the kids have "adjusted" to the divorce, but I know kids don't ever really adjust. They survive. I'm sure that our wedding will be a tough one for them. When their biological mom gets married it will be equally difficult. My parents' divorce has helped me to be the "older" kid for Jim's kids because I understand.

I feel blessed to have gone through such a trial because now God is turning it into a blessing for others. It is amazing how God "works all things together for good."

CONCLUSION

You may not have realized that grief counseling is part of a stepmom's job description. We hope this chapter revealed the many sides of childhood grief. (It may have also reminded you of your own childhood losses.) It's possible to feel overwhelmed by the magnitude of the pain your stepchildren are experiencing. This may intimidate you. A stepmom cannot heal the broken and wounded heart of a stepchild, but God can. I (Laura) know this to be true from personal experience. Your heavenly Father is not a stranger to grief or loss. Invite his wisdom and compassion to be your guide, and he can mold you into a blessing for your stepkids.

Additional Grief Counselor Interventions

Besides emotional coaching, consider these tips on helping children cope with loss.

- Keep touch points alive. Your husband should continue rituals that express love and not let the new family interrupt them. This communicates, "You still have me." For example, if as a single parent Dad lay in bed for a few minutes with his child at night, he should continue that ritual.

- Compartmentalize. At times, step back and let your husband spend one-on-one time with his children. This reduces their perceived loss of Dad.

- See the big picture. It may be irritating to watch your husband make concessions with his ex-wife on behalf of the children (not always, but when necessary), but if this reduces excessive conflict, it helps the children. Ironically, less between-home rivalry improves your standing in the family as well.

PRAYER

Lord, I admit that I've been so wrapped up in my own pain, isolation, and fear that I haven't taken the time to understand my stepchildren. Help me to learn how to be an encouragement for them. Teach me how to hear their pain, and then discern what to say and do to help them.

I believe you can create a heart in me that is pure and holy. I believe that you can turn evil around for good. And I believe that you can use me to provide a place of safety and comfort for these hurting kids. Help me to see them through your eyes, even when they say and do hurtful things to me. I desire to love them as you love them, but on my own I have no ability. I admit that fear, anger, and rejection often sabotage my efforts. Heal my heart so I may love my husband's children as you would have me do. I love you, Lord. You are my strength.

PRAYER REFERENCES

Psalm 51   *Romans 8:28*

Genesis 50:20   *Isaiah 58:11*

Smart Stepmom Discussion Questions

1. Where were you when you first heard about the 9/11 attacks? Share how you felt and how it impacted your life.

2. How does comparing your stepchildren's losses to the 9/11 attacks help you to understand their journey through pain and grief?

3. Now that you understand more about the enduring nature of grief, share an observation of your stepchildren when you witnessed:

   • developmental grieving
   • the results of cumulative impact
   • resurrected grief
   • walls of self-protection

4. How are you learning to minister to your stepchild during these occasions?

5. Review the list of ways you can respond to the walls of self-protection that stepchildren may erect.

6. Losses are experienced unequally; not everyone will react the same or need the same amount of time to grieve. In what way is this evident in your home?

7. Rate yourself on a scale of 1 to 10. How well do you emotionally coach your stepchildren? What are some ways to improve?

8. Have someone in the group read aloud Heather's long-term perspective on pages 79–80. What wisdom does she offer you?

9. This chapter may have resurrected some childhood loss issues within you. If so, consider how you might share that loss with your group; share what you have learned through it and what grieving still remains.

Chapter 5

Understanding His Kids (Part 2): Loyalty

Laurie heard David, her stepson, on the telephone with his mother.

"Last Saturday was one of my best games, Mom. You should have seen it. I had three hits—and one of them was a double."

Like many twelve-year-old boys, David had energy to spare. He was a die-hard Cubs fan and a delightful kid, and Laurie found her affection for David growing deeper than she'd expected—which is why his following words hurt so badly.

"Yeah, I had a good day at school, Mom," he continued. "I finally got a B on my history quiz!" Laurie was making stew for dinner. She wasn't trying to listen to the conversation, but he was standing in the next room, within earshot.

"She's making dinner right now." Between David's comments, Laurie pieced together the other side of the conversation. "No, not tonight. We're having soup or something. (Pause) Yeah, pretty good, I guess. I like her lasagna."

Those words of affirmation must have struck a nerve in David's mother because after the next pause he offered her words of comfort,

"No, Mom, I only call you that—I call her Buffy the Vampire Slayer."

Laurie's heart sank. *What did he just say? Buffy the Vampire Slayer? Does he really call me that? . . . I've never heard that before. . . . Does he say that behind my back? Why in the world would he say such a terrible thing? Now she's going to think I'm a terrible person and tell all her friends how wicked I am. How dare he!*

Laurie's mind raced. With her blood pressure rising and anger blazing, she slammed the spoon down and thought, *Fine, he can make his own dinner!*

LOYALTY CONFLICTS FOR CHILDREN

Loyalty is a good thing. It plants our feet securely in territory marked out for us, tells us who we belong to, and who to fight against. Offering identity and security, it's what every child (and adult) needs.

Familial loyalty is important to the health of a family because it determines priorities. For example, when a father decides not to play golf on Saturday so he can attend his daughter's athletic event, loyalty is functioning in the service of the family. When a spouse honors a date night even when work is piling up at the office, his or her devotion strengthens the family.

Loss can create steadfast loyalty (what we like to call "loyalty on steroids"). Children in stepfamilies who have experienced many losses fear even more loss. This hastens their defenses and bolsters their loyalty to biological relationships. Healthy loyalty morphs into aggressive, steadfast loyalty. When confronted with new family members, children become conflicted as they seek to balance who is considered "in" and who is not.

David didn't really think of Laurie as a vampire slayer. But his loyalty conflict between his mom and stepmom pushed him to respond to his mother as if she were in and Laurie were out.

Steadfast Loyalty to Biological Parents

Children are savagely loyal. This steadfast loyalty is not conditional or a rational, conscious choice. Even when a parent abandons a son or daughter or proves to be unreliable, a child will often remain loyal. Rooted in the God-given blood relationship between parent and child, loyalty runs as deep as DNA.

In contrast, a stepparent must earn a child's loyalty by developing emotional attachment. If honoring a stepparent means losing favor or relationship with a biological parent, the stepparent typically becomes expendable. Also, when stepfamily stress increases, children generally attempt to alleviate the tension by moving stepfamily members to the peripheral and pulling biological family members closer. The Smart Stepmom will need to find ways of tolerating this uncertainty and press through the confusion. If not, the child's "push" can feel like rejection, which may produce a feeling of hopelessness for the stepmom. One aspect to loving stepchildren is accepting that occasionally you may get the short end of the appreciation stick even when you deserve much, much more.

> ### When Mom Is Deceased
>
> One young adult said that her dad's wedding felt like another funeral for her mom. Loyalty to deceased parents can be strong, and in some cases, even more determined than loyalty to a living parent.
>
> • Children need to keep alive the memory of their mother. If loving you means risking forgetting their mother, you will find their loyalty wall very tall.
>
> • Find ways of honoring their mother and helping them to remember her significance.
>
> • Children (of all ages) experience an internal tug-of-war between loyalty to a deceased parent and a stepparent. They can imagine conversations and things the mother might/would say and find themselves "stuck" in the middle.

Emotional Tug-of-War

"Why do you have to keep fighting?" I asked every day.
I never got an answer.
It seems like it has always been this way. Since I was born.

I can't choose between you, and I won't ever do that. I love you both so much.
I was so sad when you left, Dad. My heart felt very split in half.

Chaz R., age 7
"The House Crumbles"

When biological parents are divided, children are continuously caught in an emotional tug-of-war. To side with one over the other threatens the child's security, thereby producing pain and guilt.

When biological parents are respectful of each other, the children may fear being preferential and choosing one over the other. But when parents are at war it's much worse, and the children become POWs with no safe place to lay a weary head.

Many parents are so caught up in the combat that they don't realize how often children feel caught in the middle. Other parents choose to ignore the warning signs or pain their child is suffering because they enjoy the battle. Winning is everything. It's probable that before David spoke the vampire remark his mother anxiously asked him, "Do you call Laurie 'Mom'?" Even if the question is not meant to enlist his undying allegiance, the message conveyed is, "Any affection for her threatens me; if you honor her you dishonor me." Her hidden agenda could be articulated this way: "Come over to my side by rejecting her and you'll have my complete approval." David is aware of the tenuous position between the two women. And he hears his mom's fear—and request for affirmation—loud and clear. His ultimate loyalty to his mother is well established; therefore, he is more than willing to accommodate her need. Without even knowing it, David's mother has placed him squarely in the middle of a loyalty tug-of-war.

Loyalty conflicts for children are emotionally destructive. If you or your husband are making remarks that place the kids in the war zone, it is imperative that you stop—immediately! If your husband refuses to discontinue, then you must do your part to prevent battles.

If the other home is using these tactics (or if you would like to share some of these principles with the other home for any reason), refer to the resources on Laura's Web site *www.LauraPetherbridge .com* or the e-booklet "Parenting After Divorce," found on Ron's Web site at *www.SuccessfulStepfamilies.com/co-parenting*. The page includes instructions on how to share the information with the other home. Hopefully a little insight will reduce the amount of overt loyalty tugs your stepchildren face.

Closed for the Season. Generally children who appreciate and feel affection for a stepmother fear they will anger or alienate the biological mother (or their siblings or the mother's extended family members). This creates yet another loyalty conflict when affection for you produces a problem for the child. This conflict often manifests itself as hot/cold behavior. In other words, sometimes the children are willing to let you into their lives and other times they are "closed for the season."

Loyalty conflicts may explain why children vacillate between being affectionate with you and bristling when you come near. This might also be why your name changes from time to time. A child may call you Mom until returning from Mom's house. The sadness and confusion of being with Mom and then leaving her may result in your name changing to Julie for a few days, then back to Mom. Don't take the "name game" personally.

Smart Dating

Because dating is inconsistent with actual stepfamily life, loyalty conflicts may not be evident until after the wedding. Keep in mind:

• Dating naturally limits how much the children must share their father with you. After your date, Dad comes home to them. After the wedding, when all of you share the home, loyalty issues may increase.

• Sometimes ex-wives who said little about you before the wedding escalate their negative chatter after the wedding. This can add loyalty guilt to children.

• Therefore, move slowly toward marriage. Acceptance by the children in the early stages of dating is no guarantee of acceptance after the wedding.

Instead, understand that the child is struggling to find a way through the loyalty maze. If your spouse is forcing the kids to call you Mom and they are uncomfortable doing so, it's important to share this information with him. I (Laura) never expected my stepsons to call me Mom, largely because I am their dad's wife, not their mother.

Don't assume that a name change is the direct result of something the mother said to her children, as that may or may not be the case. In the best of circumstances, children often feel caught in the middle even when no one is placing them there. It's the nature of living in a divided family.

Different House, Different Child. Children respond to adults in a way that preserves the relationship with that adult. This includes avoiding the appearance of choosing one over the other, even if it means flip-flopping their posture. This "Jekyll and Hyde" behavior can be very confusing for the adults.

David never called Laurie "Buffy the Vampire Slayer." However, to preserve the relationship with his mom, and in an attempt to alleviate her anxiety about his fondness for Laurie, he said he did. He might turn around a few minutes later and tell Laurie how much he likes her cooking. David appears manipulative and contradictory, but in reality his behavior reveals a loving heart tempered and tormented by fear.

I (Ron) shared in *The Smart Stepfamily* a story about a five-year-old who innocently asked his stepmom if he could love her when he was with her at Dad's house, and then hate her when he was at Mom's house. This wasn't manipulation; he was trying to resolve a no-win loyalty conflict by presenting himself favorably to both sides. I (Laura) know of a mentally handicapped child caught in the tug-of-war of divorce. He knows his biological mom loathes his stepmom. So he sits in a corner repeating "good mom—bad mom" to himself because he feels positive toward his stepmom, but has been instructed by his mother to judge her otherwise.

Innocent five-year-olds and handicapped children openly admit this inner conflict; most other children do not. But nearly all children in a stepfamily face it.

To some degree this means that you and your husband should be cautious in assuming that everything you hear from the children about life in the other home is entirely accurate. Realize children may filter information with an agenda of preserving the relationship with you. Listen and verify.

When you perceive that a child is skewing information in such a way that makes you look bad, decide as a couple how to proceed. Complete unity is necessary before speaking to the child, and Dad should do most of the talking. A loving confrontation may be needed, beginning with, "We know that being in the middle stinks. We also know that sometimes you feel compelled to say things to both parents in order to show your loyalty. We understand you might feel like it's wrong siding with one parent. Is that right? [Pause for response.] When you tell your mother inaccurate stories about this home so that she will feel better, it leads to conflict between this home and your mom. Please stop. We would rather you be honest with her and with us. If you are afraid to be entirely honest with your mom, we ask you not to say negative things about us. What might you say next time?" [Then dialogue with the child to create an action plan.]

Parentified Children. Wounded adults sometimes attempt to use a child's love and affection as a salve or a cure. By demanding an undying loyalty, they place the child in a caretaker role. This selfish act places a heavy emotional burden on children. When taken to an extreme, it can cripple the child.

Miguel's ex-wife had been diagnosed with bipolar personality disorder. A chaotic person, she was unpredictable and emotionally needy. She relied on her children for many things and talked to them about her lingering romantic feelings for their father. On the other hand, Miguel and his wife, Christina, were capable, high-functioning individuals. Successful careers, structure to their home, and high expectations for the children provided a stable environment for the kids. Miguel's children lived between chaos and consistency. This contrasting lifestyle presents many challenges for children who vacillate between varying expectations.

Low-functioning parents invite excessive caretaking from children. The parent's inability to manage life communicates "I need help," and children are often more than willing to fulfill the role of caretaker for the parent. A child may go to great lengths to take care of a depressed, mentally confused, or overburdened parent. This might include checking on the parent throughout the day or week, worrying about their well-being, spending excessive time and energy looking after the parent, and even abrasiveness toward the father and stepmother (as a sign of allegiance).

> ### Were You Parentified?
>
> Children are not equipped to handle adult issues. An unnatural parental burden in childhood is often a catalyst to codependency in adulthood. In light of this, it's wise for a stepmom to evaluate her own childhood.

A child who is forced to carry an adult burden of responsibility is not easily convinced that they should let go of their low-functioning parent. They have too much invested to disengage; it becomes their role in life. This child needs a great deal of coaching from your husband or a professional counselor on how to set appropriate boundaries. This should include an understanding of the guilt they will feel if they release responsibility. Letting go will require emotional maturity and an independent self-esteem. This maturity may only come with age (adulthood). In the meantime, your role as the stepmom is to remain patient and understand the child's dilemma.

Although rare, the best solution is for the low-functioning parent to mature and take responsibility for her life. This removes the child from a caretaker role and gives him permission to be a child again, thereby releasing him to have a relationship with all parents and stepparents. If this is your situation, pray continually for the low-functioning parent to "wake-up" and change the chaos. Only then will the child be free to love in a healthy manner.

Loyalty Shifts. As with loss, loyalty conflicts in children can be ignited by family transitions, life circumstances, and changes in the emotional environment. For example, when conflict flares between Dad and the biological mom, a stepmom might feel the repercussions. Anita posted a comment on *SuccessfulStepfamilies.com*, saying, "My husband's sixteen-year-old daughter was so sweet until her mother took my husband to court for more money. Since then she has had a negative attitude. She is rude, disrespectful, and treats the other kids terribly. This has caused turmoil in our house."

Changes in residence and age can also prompt loyalty shifts. Sue shared, "We have been married nine years, and I bonded with my stepchildren rather quickly as they were very young (three and six). This year my stepdaughter moved in with us. To my great surprise and shock, her attitude toward me radically changed. What once was a loving relationship is now strained."

When stress increases, children clamp down on their primary loyalties in an effort to add stability and control to their lives. The shift in attitude will likely hurt you; try to look past the immediate behavior to the insecurity beneath.

HELPING CHILDREN COPE

Children have more than enough love for all parents and family members. Helping children cope with the emotional tug-of-war begins when you, as well as all parental figures, remember that you are not in competition for the child's loyalty. If you feel insecure about your place in a child's life, refrain from allowing it to determine your significance. Handle that matter with God, your spouse, and trusted friends. Your stepchild is not responsible for your well-being. And you are not responsible for the maturity of the other adults involved.

Affirm Primary Loyalties

Saying to your stepchildren, "If I were you, my first loyalty would be to my mom," validates their feelings. It also reveals that you are not in competition with the biological mother. Stepchildren (especially adult stepchildren) typically respect and respond positively to this quality in a stepmother (though they may not communicate this positive response immediately). A stepmother who competes out of insecurity is usually thought of in negative terms and actively resisted.

Speak to the Child's Circumstances

In the last chapter we encouraged you to use emotional coaching to label a child's emotions in an attempt to help them identify and manage their grief. Emotional coaching can also be a tool to describe the tug-of-war circumstances.

"I can see that you are stuck between your mom's house and ours. I hate that for you. It must be really hard having your mother and stepfather encouraging you to go to one church and youth group while we want you to go to another. That must feel like a no-win situation for you, huh?" For children who aren't able to verbalize this tug-of-war feeling, this puts words on their experience. Older children fear discussing this dynamic because it suggests that your preference—in this case, which church to attend—may not be the only "right" one. But when you address the difficulty with compassion, it invites conversation about the predicament. Over time this facilitates trust and emotional closeness.

A related idea is to empower children with a language or code that informs you when they are feeling caught in the middle. I (Ron) worked with one father and stepmother who didn't realize how often their ten-year-old son, Juan, felt conflicted when his father and mother talked. They had a tumultuous ex-spouse relationship that often erupted in Little League parking lots and at school functions.

Juan loved baseball, so I proposed a plan. Like Juan's third-base coach, we worked out a non-verbal hand signal that Juan could give his father when he felt his anxiety rising. This signaled his father that Juan was feeling stuck in the middle and needed some relief. Juan's father learned to stop whatever was causing the anxiety at the moment and became much more sensitive to how he inadvertently put Juan in tough situations. Most important, the signal gave Juan power in his circumstances and reduced his burden.

Celebrate Joy and Relationship in the Other Home

Celebrate the other home whenever you can. When a stepmom is offended by the joys of the other home, it produces a loyalty conflict for the kids. Instead say something like, "I'm so glad your mom and stepdad took you to the amusement park on vacation! Tell me all about it." Resist the urge to defend yourself or use the moment as a weapon to vent your anger: "We would have taken you ourselves but since we pay your mom so much child support we just can't afford it. Her boyfriend has one of those 'high-and-mighty' jobs and makes lots of money, but he's not better than we are." This sort of sarcastic defensiveness loudly communicates to your stepchild that sharing joys from the other home creates anxiety. The child is made to feel guilty for enjoying special times with their mother. As a result he or she will attempt to reduce the tension between homes by shutting down and not sharing in the future.

I (Laura) was in high school when my dad shared that he and my stepmom were having a baby. I was certain that my mom would be furious; therefore, I never told her. For a long time I walked around in fear and constant tension wondering when she would find out. That pressure was almost as stressful as the news itself.

Helping children anticipate important family events is another form of celebration. Assist the child with an anniversary card to give the mother and stepfather or a birthday gift for a sibling. This

communicates to the child that you are allowing them to take pleasure in relationships associated with the other home. It demonstrates
a gracious spirit on your part and gives them permission to love.
This also communicates to your husband that you understand the
complexities facing his child, and that you desire to ease the pain.

Speak Well of Their Mom

Did you ever notice that it's okay for you to say something
negative about a family member, but if an outsider bashes them you
immediately come to their defense? In the same manner, a child's
loyalty to his or her mother will shift into overdrive if you speak
negatively about her. Plus, you inadvertently validate any ill words
the mother might have already spoken about you. If you have a
negative comment to make, make sure to say it outside the earshot
of the children.

Helping children to hold their mother close is another way of
"speaking well" of her. One stepmother thought she was strengthening the relationship with her stepchildren when she made a rule
that they could not have any photos of their mother in the house.
She thought this would cause them to focus on the new relationship
but instead it infuriated her stepchildren. They viewed her actions
as a message of dishonor toward the biological mom. This escalated
the resistance toward the stepmother, resulting in frequent conflicts
over insignificant matters.

Encourage children to maintain appropriate connections to their
mom and do not try to dismiss her importance. If at all possible
speak well of her; if you can't, then it's best to say little.

Let the Bullet Bounce

Negative comments toward you are almost a given. The poison-
ous words may come from the stepchildren, your husband's ex-wife,

former in-laws, or friends of the first family. We have a suggestion: Let the bullet bounce.

Even when wearing a bulletproof vest, police officers who are shot in the line of duty confess that it hurts very badly. The person is often knocked off their feet, and a deep bruise results. They lived to tell the story because the bullet didn't penetrate. It bounced off. You too can choose to put on a thick shield when cruel, unfair, and hurtful comments are fired. The ammunition will emotionally knock you off your feet and leave bruises, but only you decide whether it will kill you or your marriage.

This is a perfect example of how to use God's truth about your identity as a shield. You are a loved, forgiven child of the King. Even when you don't feel like it, or someone is voicing words to the contrary, you are beloved royalty. Isaiah 43:1, 4 says, "Do not fear, for I have redeemed you; I have called you by name; you are Mine! . . . Since you are precious in My sight, since you are honored and I love you . . ." (NASB). Find refuge in this truth and act accordingly.

> ## When Mom Is Deceased
>
> Don't offend adult step-children by implying that you have "replaced" their mother. This stirs a defensiveness and resistance toward you.
>
> • Celebrate her memory and special abilities.
>
> • Provide an opportunity to lay claim to family heirlooms that have sentimental value.
>
> • Tell your stepgrandchildren stories about the deceased grandmother; this sustains the family story and honors her legacy and family history.
>
> • Think of yourself as a new in-law to the family, not a mother to the children.

But don't stop there. If you really want the mind of Christ, pray for those who speak evil of you. Jesus put it this way, "You have heard that it was said, 'Love your neighbor and hate your enemy.' But I tell you: Love your enemies and pray for those who persecute you, that you may be sons of your Father in heaven" (Matthew 5:43–45). Godly love demonstrates itself in countless simple acts of kindness and graciousness—and sometimes thick skin—all of which stand as a testimony to everyone that you are a child of the Father.

With that said, let us now speak to self-protection. Putting on a bulletproof vest does not mean you should passively stand as someone's target. Finding the strength to bear up under the harsh words and praying for your persecutor does not mean you have to passively let someone abuse you. Feel free to physically remove yourself from a harsh situation or speak directly to the person: "Stop. You may not speak to me that way. If you want to discuss an issue, I am more than happy to work through it with you, but you may not criticize or judge me that way." If they will not stop, remove yourself from the situation. Be sure to communicate with your husband and create a plan to help shield your heart from future attacks.

Sometimes Take the Short End of the Stick

A Smart Stepmom knows this sacrifice may be necessary at times. For example, stepchildren who are frequently placed in loyalty conflicts by the other home need your permission to appear disloyal to you in order to prevent disapproval or anger from the other household. Sometimes love chooses the short end of the stick. Many stepchildren simply don't have the strength or ability to stand up for you; there is too much at stake. Removing them from the middle and alleviating their guilt is a gift they won't forget. And the heavenly Father, who sees what is done in secret, will offer reward (see Matthew 6:1–4).

CHALLENGING SITUATIONS

The amount of time spent with stepchildren and the emotional climate between homes can add unique challenges for some stepmothers. Here we tackle two common situations that may impact your life.

Part-Time Stepchildren

In the Crockpot of your life, ingredients that are periodically removed and returned just don't cook as fast as others. Children who have primary residence with the mother and spend weekends or occasional visits with you may need more time to bond. In this circumstance don't be surprised if the process is "one step forward, two steps back." The visits may be awkward at first—as if you've started over—but this should improve as time passes. Just recognize that it's normal for the cooking process to take longer.

If the children live a distance away and they don't get to see Dad very often, when they visit remember to give your husband and his kids as much time together as possible. Children need their father more than they need a close relationship with you. In divorce recovery ministry, the most common thing kids say when a parent moves away is, "I only get my dad for two weeks a year, and I want that time to be with him, not his new wife and kids."

Breaking Down Walls: Highly Resistant and Defiant Children

A low to moderate level of resistance toward stepmothers is common. Some stepmothers, however, find the children highly resistant or purposefully disruptive.

"His daughter Emily refuses to spend the night with us when it's our weekend. Basically she doesn't want to be with us at all," Christy shared. "I hate that for my husband. He is miserable, I miss her, and we don't know what to do." Christy and her husband previously enjoyed a strong relationship with his three children, but during adolescence, something shifted Emily's loyalties. "I know she wants to be with her friends," Christy continued, "but I also think she is avoiding me for some reason." We offered Christy a few suggestions.

- *Let compassion lead.* Generally, highly resistant children are protesting their circumstances (e.g., persistent anger at parents for divorcing) or reflecting an inner loyalty conflict. If they can't make everyone happy, some children will choose the lesser of the evils and not engage anyone at all. Being angry toward the child or becoming a victim makes things worse. Emotional coaching skills may help to speak to the circumstances, but the reality is you may hit a brick wall.

- *Give the child a safe outlet.* The child who withdraws from the stepfamily might not be willing to discuss their loss or loyalty conflicts with you or your husband, but they may tell someone else they trust. A grandparent or another relative may be able to discuss the issue with them. Sometimes, though, a counselor is the only truly neutral person with whom a child feels safe enough to work through their turmoil.

- *Capitalize on your middle ground* (see chapter 1). Focus on the activities or interests that naturally connect the two of you. One mom shared that her difficult stepdaughter loved Starbucks, so when they ran an errand together it was a perfect time for a few minutes together. Make the most of what you have, when you have it.

- *Pursue with gentleness.* A child who limits contact with your home should not be badgered. Pestering the child makes him or her run faster; patience is the key. Choose convenient opportunities to create contact.

- *Keep the door open.* Children who for a season of life remove themselves from you or your husband will sometimes be open to contact in a new season. Don't completely close the door just because they may have done so to you. Reconciling relationships is at the very heart of God.

- *Allow them alone time with their dad.* If a child boycotts you but is open to time with Dad, it's best to accommodate him or her to keep the contact alive. Your husband should not cater to this entirely, but occasional time with the child is better than nothing. This can be balanced with gentle nudging from your husband to include you at some point.

- *Speak up for decency.* A child who is highly disrespectful to you or disruptive of your lifestyle should experience consequences from your husband. You should speak up for yourself also. One courageous stepmother who knew that her husband would be supportive told her troubled nineteen-year-old stepson, "Do not speak to me that way. You don't have to love me or share our values, but you may not treat me like that. Also, you may not barge into our house in the middle of the night. Call before you come over." Couple unity is of supreme importance in a situation like this; be sure to negotiate expectations with your husband so you can respond with confidence (see chapter 8).

- *Sometimes letting go creates much needed space.* Cindy's story demonstrates the wisdom of backing off when resistance continues.

I was ignored by my oldest stepdaughter (age nine) for a long time. She really didn't speak to me for the first few years, not even a hello or good-bye. We spent many nights trying to get to the root of the problem. What we discovered was that her bitter mom was saying horrible things about me. I realized I couldn't control her mom's behavior, so I eventually let it all go. I decided that my day was not going to be determined by whether or not my stepdaughter said please or thank you. It was very hard at first, but as I distanced myself and pulled back, she slowly stepped forward. And I mean slowly. It's been five years and at this point we exchange basic daily communication.

The turning point for Cindy was in deciding not to let her stepdaughter's resistance dictate her mood or responses. Ironically, changing her part of the dance and lowering her expectations created space for the stepdaughter to step forward. Five years is a long time to wait. But there is reward in patience.

FINAL THOUGHTS

After divorce or the death of a mom, matters of loss and loyalty get played out in a child's life nearly every single day. Recognizing the issues and learning how to respond in a way that builds a bridge are key components to building a healthy stepfamily.

PRAYER

Dear Lord, I confess that I often view my stepkids as the enemy. They create stress in our home, and I'm resentful. But I praise you for helping me to understand why my stepchild acts in ways that are hurtful to me. The clarity helps me to comprehend their pain. The Bible tells me that patience helps to strengthen my heart. Teach me how to love children who may feel disloyal to their mom if they love me back. Help me to hug kids who act like porcupines. It's going to take supernatural strength and divine insight to be a Smart Stepmom. But I surrender to your guidance, and I trust you.

Lord, I often feel like a failure at all of this, but I desire to take your hand and let you lead me. Help me to love my husband by responding to his children in a way that builds relationship. Your Word tells me to refrain from speaking destructive words; therefore, help me to know when to keep silent. Show me when and how to adapt my responses depending on the circumstance. I desire to be flexible and teachable.

Like a little child, I now crawl onto your lap, lay my weary head against your chest, and allow your heartbeat to comfort me. You are my heavenly Daddy, and you are big enough to handle everything. Amen.

PRAYER REFERENCES

2 John 1:3
James 5:7–8
Psalm 34:13

James 3:5–12
Psalm 131:1–2

Smart Stepmom Discussion Questions

1. How do your stepkids behave or what do they say that causes discouragement or disruption in your home?

2. Loyalty is an important factor for the family because it helps to set priorities. However, in stepfamilies it can be problematic and cause division. Share ways you might cope with both aspects.

3. It's normal for children to be savagely loyal to their mothers. What steps can you take to show your stepchildren that you understand their need to protect and comfort their mom?

4. Are there steps you can take to build mutual loyalty between you and your husband's kids?

5. In what ways do you observe your stepchildren experiencing an emotional tug-of-war? How is that battle affecting the family? Is there something you can suggest to your husband that might ease the stress?

6. Which of these dynamics are at play in your family? Refer back to the chapter to explore each.

   • Closed for the Season
   • Different House, Different Child
   • Parentified Children
   • Loyalty Shifts

7. Are you dealing with a highly resistant child? What are a few steps you could take to reach out to him or her?

8. Review the section entitled Helping Children Cope on pages 91–96. Which challenging situations are pushing you to the breaking point? What strategies might you implement to help ease the situation?

Chapter 6

Partnering: Stepparenting Beside the Engaged or Disengaged Father

The power that guilt has over divorced parents is huge. As a child, my husband experienced the divorce of his parents. Therefore, he sympathizes with the plight of his children as they adjust to new stepparents and surroundings. His children manipulate situations so that they wreak havoc on our household. There always seems to be a deeper psychological meaning to everything and an excuse for their poor behavior and lack of respect. Why am I the only one who sees this?
Mary

Mary isn't the only stepmother married to a man burdened with guilt. Raising children into mature adults requires an incredible amount of hard work and cooperation between a husband and wife. For a stepfamily to be successful it is imperative that the dad be an active participant. If your husband is engaged in parenting his children in your home, the role of stepmother becomes much easier. If he isn't, the opposite is true. When fathers like Mary's husband excuse poor behavior or become paralyzed by guilt, stepmothers experience defeat.

You may be prepared and determined to tackle the challenges of being a stepmother, but without your husband's support, it's almost impossible. This chapter is designed to help a stepmom understand why and how a dad disengages from active parenting. It also examines your role and how to work alongside a paralyzed parent. The next two chapters, written for both you and your husband, help you discover your roles as parents and how to be a united team.

THE ENGAGED FATHER

Shondra's husband, Jerry, took being a father very seriously. He talked with and listened to his kids, took proactive steps to communicate expectations for their behavior, set limits, and enforced consequences when they crossed the line. Jerry was far from the perfect parent, but he worked hard. His children respected him and had a healthy reverence for adults in general. This made Shondra's entrance as a stepmom relatively painless. Her stepchildren didn't immediately embrace her, but they did treat her courteously. Because Jerry had been a proactive parent, it took a while for him to make room for Shondra's input on parenting decisions. At first she didn't feel needed, but eventually he allowed her to become part of the team; they talked frequently about the children and negotiated decisions together. When action was necessary, Jerry would take the initiative to communicate their expectations to his children and then followed through with a reasonable punishment when the kids disobeyed. Jerry's initiative took Shondra out of the position of being the heavy and, therefore, created space for her to develop a relationship with the stepchildren. Over the years the marriage matured, and her authority as a parent figure increased.

THE DISENGAGED FATHER

Kim's husband, Tony, on the other hand, rarely engaged his children. A conscientious and hard worker, Tony provided financially for his family; however, ethical and spiritual leadership were not his strength. He wasn't emotionally connected with his children, nor did he discipline them. Tony had good intentions as a parent, but he fell short of actually doing what was best.

Kim's children were adults, ages nineteen and twenty-two. Over the years she learned practical lessons about parenting. On the surface Tony welcomed her suggestions because he recognized his inconsistencies. He and Kim naïvely assumed she would walk into the new family and turn things around. There was just one problem—she couldn't. Each time Kim took the initiative to raise the standard of conduct in the home, Tony's kids would complain to him that it wasn't fair or that she was too impatient. Tony responded by taking one of two positions: he defended his kids' good intentions, or he opposed the new standard that Kim was trying to accomplish. If the couple had previously communicated and agreed on the expectations, Tony reverted back to his former ways and wouldn't follow through. Kim was undermined and frustrated.

> ### Smart Dating
>
> During courtship it's very important to observe how a man parents his children. Blinded by the fog of love, it's not uncommon for a woman to minimize the patterns of a disengaged dad. Realize that his lack of parenting creates huge issues for your future should you marry him. The consequence of ignoring these traits is a marriage filled with stress, turmoil, and disagreements. If you don't agree with his parenting style and he is unwilling to change, it may be best to reevaluate the relationship or delay marriage. If you do not, understand that you are stepping into a very difficult situation.

One could argue that Tony was an engaged father because he was financially and physically present; however, in reality he was disengaged in the actual process of training, exhorting, and disciplining his children. Without his active participation, Kim's ability to positively influence his children was sabotaged. She learned that without the father's support, trying to parent his kids is like—as one stepmother said—"Setting your hair on fire and putting it out with a hammer!" [1]

UNDERSTANDING THE DISENGAGED FATHER

My husband is lenient with his kids and treats them like they are babies. He serves them hand and foot, expecting little in return. This results in major dissension.
Tricia

If you are living with an engaged father, there may be frustrations, but it's likely that you aren't being sabotaged by his parenting. Sometimes frustration arises because your husband took the initiative to set boundaries with his kids and didn't discuss it with you first. Gently share your concern and that you'd like to be informed in the future, but count your blessings. Many stepmoms would be thrilled to have a husband who is willing to allow his kids to suffer a consequence when they make poor choices. After reading about the plight of stepmoms with disengaged husbands, you might want to show your appreciation to your spouse by giving him a big gratitude kiss. You will learn additional tips to partnering with him in the next few chapters.

If you are married to a disengaged dad, you may find yourself thinking of him as the enemy. This will stir bitterness and disrespect in your heart. My (Laura's) husband's inability to hold his kids accountable caused me to view him as anemic and weak. What I didn't understand was that my husband wasn't ignoring the behavior on purpose; he just didn't know what to do to correct the situation. Instead of helping my spouse, my lack of knowledge caused me to withdraw. Learn alternative ways of responding that promote change. Sometimes both spouses need to ask for forgiveness, for example, but don't ignore issues or rude, neglectful behavior.

If a father is open to learning, a loving, respectful stepmom can help him to become a better disciplinarian. If the stepmom is heavy-handed, overly critical, or controlling, she loses her influence. Acknowledging your husband's struggles and asking God to help you understand the reasons behind his actions is the first step toward becoming a part of the solution rather than fuel on the fire. Your husband will be more open to constructive suggestions once he knows you desire to understand his circumstances and identify with his pain.

Puzzled, Paralyzed, and Fighting Castration

Disengaged fathers aren't stupid or unloving. They feel as much compassion for their children as engaged fathers, but the process of engagement has been short-circuited. You may be surprised to know that nearly all fathers struggle with the bewilderment of parenting, but the disengaged dad also battles guilt, which can paralyze him. He may also fear relational castration by you. Allow us to explain.

Puzzled Fathers. Fathers with little education about child development, discipline, punishment, and the spiritual development of children often feel puzzled about how to parent. They don't engage because they don't know how.

For years I (Ron) faked my way through conversations with other guys about cars and home maintenance. I don't have a mechanical bone in my body, and to be quite frank, I have no interest in those subjects. I just don't enjoy that stuff. Whenever the car broke down or the engine overheated, I was stuck (my wife might say "useless"). I didn't know where to begin. Furthermore, I was too embarrassed to ask for help, so I would attempt to fix the problem myself or, even worse, ignore the predicament for as long as possible.

Many men have this attitude about child rearing. It is unfamiliar territory; they don't know how to navigate the terrain, so they pull back or stumble through. The confusion is magnified if your husband's dad was a disengaged father. Typically we learn how to parent from our parents, but this dad has no role model. It's not that he doesn't care; he sincerely doesn't know what to do.

Another key point to remember is that your husband and his children have settled into his familiar style of parenting. When you desire a change, it will require more than just your spouse's cooperation; it will require adjustment from the kids also. Aggressive changes will make enemies—fast!

Early in our marriage I (Laura) wanted to implement changes for my stepkids, such as healthier eating habits. But my actions quickly turned into an unnecessary battleground. I had to learn which issues were worth tackling and which ones to let go. I had to accept that my husband and his former wife had decided to allow the kids to eat foods that I felt were unhealthy. Although I could offer healthier choices when they were at my house, it wasn't my job to change their eating habits.

Your husband may interpret your suggestions or advice as your agenda versus his, a battle for control. A wise suggestion that can defuse a potential bomb is to read a parenting book or attend a parenting class *together*. It is very important that you consider this a shared learning experience, not just something "for him." The book, author, or class teacher becomes a neutral third party who provides both of you with parenting instructions. This diminishes the battleground dynamic, keeping you on the same side. But make sure you find the right training. Parenting in stepfamilies has many unique dynamics not addressed in most parenting classes and resources written for biological families. Take advantage of such resources, but be sure to add information geared specifically toward your situation.

Paralyzed Fathers. Fathers who are large in size and stature and highly competent on the job can be wimpy with their kids. Some, like Rick, describe themselves as tired: "I work hard all day, and when I get home I just don't have the energy to discipline my kids. To be honest, getting them to finish their chores doesn't seem like a big deal." This father is paralyzed by fatigue.

Other dads are paralyzed by fear. They are afraid to set limits because then the biological mother's home will become more appealing to the children. This dad may fear, for example, another trip to family court if his former wife doesn't approve of his parenting; therefore, he tiptoes around the issues.

Yet other fathers are paralyzed by what parenting expert John Rosemond calls "psychological thinking."[2] These dads spend an inordinate amount of time trying to analyze why the child misbehaves. "What does it mean?" is this parent's most asked question. The fact that sixteen-year-old Susie can't get her assignments turned in at school is not a lack of responsibility, but rather a symbolic mystery the parent must figure out. Furthermore, for this parent, punishing a child for something that is about some "deeper psychological need" doesn't seem fair.

> ### When Mom Is Deceased
>
> The loss of a spouse is devastating. In its wake, formerly engaged fathers can become passive, paralyzed parents. For example, in an attempt to console children, fathers may lower their behavioral standards to protect a child from more pain. This is understandable given the circumstances, so be careful not to judge him. Instead, ask how he parented before versus after the loss. Encourage him to parent with strength as he once did.

Rosemond points out that unfortunately our society as a whole is shifting toward this parenting mentality. But your husband's temptation to parent in this manner is even greater because guilt often causes parents to overlook disobedience and become overly sympathetic toward their children. Fathers may feel guilty that the kids are suffering due to multiple losses, emotional pain, and even your marriage. This dad understands that for him the marriage brought happiness, but for his children it may have added to their confusion and loss. In addition, if a dad made immoral choices that caused a divorce, his shame may overshadow his parental reasoning.

Noncustodial dads who have occasional weekend visitation can be completely paralyzed by guilt if the entire weekend isn't a positive experience. Confronting a child's bad behavior alters the mood, which may seem like a costly and foolish decision to the dad when his time with the kids is so limited.

Giving your husband the "you don't have to feel guilty" speech is unwise because it minimizes his feelings. His emotions may be irrational, but it's likely he doesn't want to hear sensible, cognitive-based arguments. Think back to the last time someone suggested that you shouldn't feel a certain way. It usually makes us angry. A more productive approach is to encourage your spouse to talk about the guilt. Share that you are reading a book on this subject, and apologize for the insensitivity of your former comments. Calmly discuss how guilt may be affecting his parenting decisions and behavior. Hopefully this will prompt him to ask you about the book and you can share the chapters designed for both of you. Pray for him to recognize the danger of allowing guilt to dictate his parenting, and ask God to reveal any deeper reasons why he is paralyzed.

Fighting Castration. I (Ron) will never forget one stepcouple counseling session. Angela had been a stepmom to Robert's two children for five years. But she was really frustrated. "He asks my opinion about things and then ignores it. I don't understand why he won't listen to me."

I asked Robert why he was resistant to Angela's advice.

"I'm not sure," he replied. (Pause) "The man stuff, I guess."

"What do you mean by 'man stuff'?" I asked.

"You know, wanting to be tough, independent, and strong for my kids. I don't like feeling pushed around. Everywhere I turn there's a woman trying to tell me what to do—my ex-wife, my mother, my ex-mother-in-law, my wife, even my daughters. It feels like everyone is trying to castrate me."

They use different words, but through the years I've heard a lot of men discuss their "man stuff." Even in marriage many men work hard to keep their psychological independence (so they're not "whipped" by their wife). These men don't reveal many of their thoughts or feelings for fear of being exposed. As one man put it, "If she's like my ex-wife, she'll just use it against me later." This is how men view protecting their "man stuff."

Ladies, this next statement may take a few minutes to sink in: A man who feels controlled by his wife will fight castration with every bone in his body. Combat will ensue. I realize that the intent of most women is not to castrate their husbands, but some men will interpret your actions that way.

"That's so childish," you might protest. "It's all just masculine pride." To a degree, and for some men, that's true. They bought the lie that staying on top in marriage is the only way to keep your male dignity. It's not true, but our society orients men to think in that manner. Sometimes the church fuels this perception by perverting the word *submission* into meaning domination.

For other men, however, this "man stuff" isn't as much about pride as it is about survival and emotional safety. Ironically, the tough external shield this guy holds is protecting an inner soft, tender center that is deeply afraid. For example, a man who was disrespected by a former wife may fear intense criticism in a second marriage.

Another dad fears that his children will suffer because he can't protect them. One man had deep anxiety remembering his own father's words, "You'll never amount to anything." He fears his dad might be right. This causes him to construct barriers of self-protection such as hiding, withdrawing, becoming defensive, or aggressively shutting out his wife. The man who fears emotional castration will do anything to avoid a woman's knife.

Many women don't deserve this level

> ### For Those With Adult Stepchildren
>
> Even if his children are out of the house, any negative comments you make about their life or choices implies criticism of his parenting. Offer compliments when you can and look for ways to affirm who his children have become. When you can't say something complimentary, approach him with gentleness and humility.

of guardedness from their husband, but others castrate their husband without even realizing it.

For many years I (Laura) didn't realize that I tampered with my husband's "man stuff." I was raised in a home by a single mom who worked very hard and was extremely independent. Growing up I often heard that men were weak, and I was totally unaware that this had produced a negative view of men. When my husband didn't hold his kids accountable, it triggered those distorted childhood messages lodged in the recesses of my mind. To me he was spineless, and my respect for him dwindled to zero. All I wanted to do was run from the situation. His wimpiness (in my opinion) made me nauseous. I'm ashamed to admit that I said cruel and hurtful words to my sweet husband. A misunderstanding of why he wasn't taking control, combined with my distorted view of men, created toxic results.

It's extremely important to understand that the relationship you had with your parents, in particular your father, plus the childhood messages you received while growing up, can have an overwhelming effect on your role and attitude as a wife. In addition, if you were previously married and it wasn't a healthy relationship, you may be carrying hidden issues that can affect your present marriage. Explore these issues so you can minimize their impact on how you treat your husband. For example, if you have been divorced we highly recommend that you read Laura's book *When "I Do" Becomes "I Don't": Practical Steps for Healing During Separation and Divorce*. My upbringing, coupled with a painful divorce, created deep wounds in my life. These issues had to be healed before I was able to learn how to honor and respect my husband. Uncovering the pain was a difficult process, but eventually I was able to support my spouse as a Christian woman should.

As agonizing as it might be, take a moment to evaluate your reactions. How would your husband describe your attitude toward him? If you are responding the way I did, your words may be devastating to your husband. This doesn't build a marriage; it tears the union apart. Take the necessary steps to discover why you are inflicting pain on your spouse rather than encouraging him.

Whether or not you find anything to change about yourself, it's important to understand these principles:

- If your husband has ever had a woman try to castrate him (ex-wife, his mother, past girlfriend, etc.), he will be sensitive to any behavior from you that mimics what he experienced before. Even if you don't mean to be controlling or bossy, he might perceive you in this way. His battles are his problem; it's not your job to change him. He must get help on his own, but it's important to refrain from exacerbating the issue.

- A man who feels like his wife is trying to control him will never let her close enough to love him. He will keep her at arm's length, and she will wonder why he is disconnected.

- Demonstrating respect toward your husband is a great motivator for him. Showing appreciation for your spouse restores his sense of safety and security, thereby lowering his defenses. If he feels safe, he will allow you closer. This may also ignite a leadership role as a father and encourage his initiative as a parent.[3]

STEPPARENTING BESIDE THE DISENGAGED FATHER

A man who is puzzled, paralyzed, or fighting castration is not parenting from a strong position. Chapters seven and eight, designed for your husband, encourage him to identify problems and implement necessary changes. This section informs a stepmom of her role.

First, clearly grasp that you are not responsible to fix, change, or heal your husband's struggles. When a woman takes on the responsibility of helping her husband change or overcome his fears, her actions often take on the appearance of control. When this occurs, the husband responds with resistance or defense, making her efforts futile. He labels his wife "controlling," and she responds with "stubborn." The answer is to recognize and resist the urge to fix or rescue your spouse! It's not your job—it's God's job, and he is more than capable.

Responding to a disengaged father is not easy! It takes intentional effort and wise insight bathed in humility. Here are four key elements to parenting beside him.

Examine Your Part of the Dance

First, examine past interactions and your part in your parental "dance." All couples, happy and miserable, have a cycle of steps— or dance—that influences how they interact with each other. Some steps bring us closer together (such as acts of thoughtfulness), and other steps separate (acts of selfishness). Certain strides build walls in the marriage (criticism), and others break through the fortress (forgiveness).

Typically a husband or wife views the sequence of steps in the marriage dance from his or her own perspective. As a therapist, when a couple comes to me for counseling, I (Ron) often observe the husband listing all of the negative things that his wife does or says. Then the wife shares her side of the story, which puts the blame on him. Who's right? They both are. If you put the two stories together, they reveal a dance that is mutually negative and mutually blaming.

Scott has four children from a previous marriage. He and his second wife, Shelly, have one child together. To Shelly's dismay, Scott does not discipline his four older children in the same manner that he does their child. He lives in constant fear that his ex-wife will take him back to court, so he doesn't rock the boat. Shelly has lost respect for her spouse and becomes frustrated with him, especially when his lack of follow-through results in the kids' unwillingness to help around the house. Her anger is causing her to emotionally pull away from him. When he initiates sex, she has no desire. He feels rejected and gets angry with her for not "wanting it" like she used to. The more he demands sex, the more she feels used; the more she insists that he change, the more he accuses her of being difficult. Scott and Shelly each have a perspective of what is wrong with the relationship. Until each spouse recognizes and admits how his or her individual actions mutually support this negative dance, the destructive pattern will continue.

In your marriage, observe what you do prior to your husband's negative actions. For example, Shelly is aware that Scott is extremely defensive about his children. Guilt from the past combined with fatherly efforts to protect his kids has produced a paralyzed parent. Scott is parenting from vulnerability instead of strength. Therefore, Shelly would be wise to take this into consideration before approaching him with a complaint about his children. A critical and condescending tone may ignite his shame and defensiveness. Proverbs 15:1 can provide Shelly with the wisdom she needs: "A gentle answer turns away wrath, but a harsh word stirs up anger." It's not Shelly's job to cure Scott's defensiveness or his inability to discipline his children, but if family harmony is desired, she'll need to change her approach.

In addition to being paralyzed, Scott has been fighting castration and low self-worth for some time. His previous marriage inflicted deep wounds of rejection, control, and inadequacy. If Shelly punches his bruise with harsh words, he is likely to react with anger and defensiveness. Shelly's critical tone is not the cause for his defensiveness; his previous wounds are. However, her nasty words throw gasoline on a burning flame. This cycle will continue until Scott gets help for his past hurts and Shelly learns how to respond without anger.

Reach Him With Humility

What is humility? If you are like me (Laura), it doesn't sound very appealing. In the past I've been hurt by those I trusted. Therefore, before I fully understood the definition of humility, the word stirred fear in my heart. I assumed if I became humble that I'd be weak and people would take advantage of me. But a dictionary explains that a humble person is one who is "not proud or haughty: not arrogant." In other words, a humble woman doesn't view herself as superior to others; she isn't prideful. Humility is not weakness; it is strength.

This is the posture that Christ so exquisitely demonstrated in his lifetime: "Your attitude should be the same as that of Christ Jesus: Who, being in very nature God, did not consider equality with God something to be grasped, but made himself nothing, taking the very nature of a servant, being made in human likeness. And being found in appearance as a man, he humbled himself and became obedient to death—even death on a cross!" (Philippians 2:5–8).

Have you ever noticed that people are turned off by arrogance and are attracted to humility? That's because a humble heart demonstrates the character of Christ. Humility lessens hurts, opens emotions, and creates safety in relationships because it does not look to satisfy its own interests but those of others. Humility is so powerful that it softens the heart of God. Throughout Scripture the one attitude that awakens his grace is humility: "God opposes the proud but gives grace to the humble" (James 4:6).

A humble heart increases your voice because a husband is much more likely to hear your viewpoint. Humility gently invites his listening ear rather than igniting his defenses. Imagine changing a conversation from "Why do you turn a deaf ear to your son's misbehavior?" to "I know I used to be very critical of your parenting and of your son. I own that, and I'm sorry. I certainly am not a perfect parent and don't have all the answers. I am concerned that

Braden is taking advantage of you and learning some poor habits that will not serve him well in life. Are you open to hearing my point of view?"[4] The former is dripping with criticism and arrogance. It implies that you have *the* answer and your husband ought to listen to you. The latter approach begins with humility and an admission of your previous negative behavior. This identifies your part of the dance and clearly communicates that you are taking responsibility for it. Once that is established, it becomes easier to bridge into the topic at hand.

Demonstrating humility when you are frustrated is extremely difficult. You may feel betrayed by your husband's lack of investment in his children and resentful that your role in the family has been disregarded and disrespected. This unselfish act will require prayer, power from the Holy Spirit, and support from friends. Sometimes God uses frustrating circumstances to increase our faith and dependence upon him; it is often how we become more like Christ.

The reason many stepmoms fail with humility is because they try the "white knuckle" approach with their own strength and ability. They try to "grin and bear it" as long as humanly possible, and the outcome is short-lived. To obtain long-term results, the key is to learn how to obtain the mind of Christ and allow the Holy Spirit to transform your thinking. He is more than willing to replace destructive thoughts with positive ones (Romans 12:1–2). A willing heart is what he seeks.

Don't Flip-Flop Emotions: Articulate Your Goals and Desires for His Children

When parenting beside a disengaged father, you may catch yourself attacking your spouse for a simple issue when the deeper reasons are worry or disconnectedness. For example, it's common to nitpick when inside the battle is loneliness. I (Ron) like to call this an emotional flip-flop. We flip one emotion with another. Usually the emotion that gets flipped is a softer, more vulnerable one. The one we replace it with (the "flop") is typically hard and aggressive. Another example is protesting your husband's paralyzed responses to his children with angry criticism (the "flop") when what you really feel (the "flip") is fear that they will continue making poor choices and suffer many consequences.

And what is a partner's typical response to a hard, aggressive emotional response? That's right, they flip-flop too. They may feel hurt inside by your words, but they flip that softer emotion for a hard, defensive response. Pretty soon both partners are flopping negative responses back and forth. It's war!

When a stepmother addresses a stepchild's behavior, it may come across as condemnation when what she is really attempting to express is concern for the child's well-being. "Rachel is a slob," Michelle would say to her husband. "She doesn't clean up after herself, and you don't seem to care. You just expect me to do all the work." This statement is full of accusation and criticism of her husband's parenting ability and his daughter. Sadly, Michelle's words don't express her genuine heart for Rachel. A better communication could include, "Jason, I want you to know that I do care about Rachel, and I want her to have a productive future. I'm not sure we're helping her to prepare for adulthood when we don't hold her accountable. Can we talk about this?" Until a husband trusts that his wife genuinely cares about his child, he won't hear a word said. He'll just believe that you are unfairly criticizing his child or trying to castrate him. Repeatedly show that you desire good things for his child; this will motivate him to listen.

Accept What You Cannot Change

Right now I feel like I'm expected to act as their mom, but I'm not allowed to actually be their mom. Does that make any sense?

Lisa

A husband's support is the foundation upon which a stepmom builds parental authority. It is his job to dictate to his kids that they honor your rules. Understand that his parenting standards have already created a baseline for what his kids expect. It's almost impossible for a stepmom to raise the level of discipline and structure to a higher level than Dad's. For example, if your spouse permits his children to leave clothes scattered all over the floor, you will have an extremely difficult time changing that habit unless he raises the standard.

Unless your husband decides that he wants to see a change, don't try to implement the change yourself. Many stepmoms fall into the trap and assume it is a stepmom's responsibility to take the kids farther than a disengaged father does. This unrealistic and frustrating approach typically ends with the stepmom feeling undercut by the kids and the dad again and again. If you have already tried this strategy, step back and learn to put up with habits or behaviors that you find unappealing. The life of a stepmom often includes accepting the numerous things out of your control. It's essential to understand that a stepmom has a different role than a biological parent. Jeannie shares, "I found the strength to accept what I could not change, and it freed me from my anger. I came to realize that each day there will be issues and problems that I cannot change. What I can change is myself and the way I handle our family issues." The decision is up to you—aggravation or acceptance.

> **Stepmom Self-Care:**
>
> Letting go of what you can't change is the ultimate in self-care. Instead of insisting on change you don't have the power to facilitate, work within the power or authority you do have. Don't blame yourself when he doesn't step out as far as you'd like. Learn to endure frustration while everyone grows in their role.

If you feel powerless in your own home, keep this perspective. Changing your part of the dance and leading with humility, learning how to set healthy boundaries, and articulating your heart for his kids is how a stepmom gains strength and stability in the marriage. These tools provide influence in a family system that otherwise silences your voice.

This last suggestion on stepping back has a paradoxical impact that we first discussed earlier in the book, but it bears repeating here. Politely resigning, as we called it in chapter 2, helps you to relax and not feel sabotaged or defeated. Plus it requires your husband to step in and fill in the gap you left behind. This is the ultimate goal, a dad who is engaged with his kids.

Imagine humbly telling your husband, "I know I have been riding your kids about their chores for quite a while. I've taken a long, hard look at that and I've decided to let it go." Pause and then continue, "I haven't given up on your children—I still desire for them to learn how to be responsible for their things so that they will mature into capable, independent adults—but until it's something you and I can work on together, I need to let it go. I'm aware that they really seek your direction in these areas, and ultimately you have much more influence than I do as the stepmom. So I'm going to let all of this go and follow your lead for a while."

This statement is not sarcastic (humility is not manipulation), nor is it an expression of withdrawal. She merely acknowledges that a stepmom can only step into the position of authority that the biological dad permits. When you remove yourself as the person in charge, it can cause others to reevaluate the expectations and roles of everyone within the family. At the very least it moves a disengaged dad into the primary parenting role. If and when that happens, everybody wins.

None of these suggestions guarantee a perfect marriage or a more responsive husband. We can't promise specific results, but we believe the likelihood of beneficial results increases significantly if you implement these ideas. Keep your eyes on Christ. He desires a strong, healthy marriage and family for you even more than you do.

PRAYER

Dear God, I'm tired of stepping into the parenting role that my husband should be filling. I desire to humbly step back, but I've been doing this for so long that I don't know how to change. Teach me the things that I can control, and help me to let go of those I can't. And show me anything I'm doing that is making the situation worse.

I know I'm sometimes nasty to my spouse and his kids. Hurtful words come out of my mouth before I even realize I'm saying them. And then I feel so ashamed. I desire to change that pattern, and I believe the Bible when it says that you can transform my mind. If I have emotional wounds that are causing me to inflict pain on others, please help me to recognize the problem and receive help.

Lord, I can't do any of this without your help; you are my strength. I trust your Word when it says that you are faithful and that you can make me holy. I place our family in your hands. Amen.

PRAYER REFERENCES

Romans 12:2   1 Thessalonians 5:23–24
Psalm 18:32

Smart Stepmom Discussion Questions

1. In what ways is your husband engaged as a father?

2. In what ways would you describe him as disengaged?

3. When are you most tempted to become bitter toward your husband regarding his parenting?

4. If your husband read this chapter, would he describe himself as puzzled, paralyzed, fighting castration, or none of the above?

5. Share one part of the parental dance where you need to take ownership and change.

6. What do you think of when you hear the word *humble*? What makes leading with humility so difficult? Share a way that you can try Christlike humility this week. Remember next week to share what you experienced.

7. If you have been undercut in your home, in what ways does stepping back in parenting sound relieving? In what ways does it sound frustrating?

8. What steps can you take this week to learn how to let go of the things you can't change?

9. Is it possible to set a specific time for you and your spouse to pray together?

Getting Smart: The Stepparenting Team

It's time to get practical. Getting smart in your role as stepmom involves the following:

- teamwork with your husband
- constructive ambassadorship with the other home
- wisdom to comprehend the motivating factors for stepchildren
- practical parenting how-to's.

This section will walk you through each of these topics.

Stepparenting is a team sport, but not all the teammates have equal influence. Your success is heavily dependent upon your husband's help, support, and partnership in parenting. We have included two chapters to help him understand. Invite your husband to read chapters 7 and 8 along with you. Doing your job pivots upon him doing his. Let's start there.

Chapter 7

Dad Smart (Part 1): She Can't Do It Without You

She can't do it without you.

You've married an incredible woman. She makes you smile, supports your work, laughs at your jokes, and has agreed to help you raise your children. How awesome is that?! The child rearing part, by the way, probably lines her up for a medal.

However, her ability to fulfill the role of stepmom is dependent upon you. If you neglect your role, she has no foundation upon which to stand. Stepparenting is a team sport. If you want your marriage to succeed, you must be her teammate and stick by her side.

FROM GOOD TO GREAT

Part of being teammates involves having similar parenting philosophies. You can't operate from two different parenting viewpoints and expect to end up on the same team. Parenting in a stepfamily functions differently than parenting in a biological family. Following our basic principles will put you on a winning team. We've included sidebars throughout this chapter that speak to different stepmom situations. These are designed to help your parenting team go from good to great.

Principle 1: Declare Loyalty to Your Wife

"I am so hurt. My husband has another woman in his life . . . and it is his daughter." To a dad this may seem ridiculous. But because a natural bond between a stepmother and daughter is absent, even a daughter may feel like the other woman. Nothing deflates a woman's heart more than feeling disposable to her husband. Furthermore, nothing will destroy your home more quickly than communicating a loyalty to your children that is greater than your loyalty to your wife. This is first on our list because the others are dependent upon this principle. In other words, united you stand, divided you fall. Declaring your loyalty has two aspects.

1. *Tell your kids.* Children need to hear you repeatedly share throughout their lifetime that you and your wife will always be together. This is not a statement of preference (your wife over your children), but a statement of *permanence*. If your children believe there's a chance that she won't be around at some point, their motivation to include her and respect her role in their lives diminishes tremendously.

2. *Show your kids.* Actions speak louder than words. If you say you are committed to your wife but undercut her when she disciplines the children, your actions contradict your words.

Cohabitation and Smart Dating

Many couples who cohabit do so for financial reasons and because they believe it is a trial marriage. Far from the safety of a committed marriage, a cohabiting relationship actually facilitates relationship decline. Research shows that cohabiting couples are less happy, more depressed, less financially supportive of each other, less sexually committed, more negative about marriage, have lower levels of premarital relationship satisfaction and, if they marry after cohabiting, have a higher divorce rate than couples who do not. This is true of those who have never been married as well as couples considering remarriage. God's boundaries around sexuality are meant to protect us from these and other damaging outcomes.[1]

If you typically let a child's opinion or mood sway your decisions more so than your wife's opinion, your actions will sabotage your wife's role in the family. You must make her a full-fledged member of the parenting team by using actions to back up your stated loyalty.

Principle 2: Trust Your Wife's Heart

Do you wonder if your wife loves your kids as much as you do? Perhaps a fight occurred or you noticed the way your wife expressed criticism about one of your children and it bothered you. You begin thinking, *Can I really trust that she cares for the well-being of my kids, or do I have to look out for them?* If you have ever had such a fear, you are not alone.

One of the givens of a biological family is that both parents feel a deep bond with their children. After all, they are flesh and blood, your little miracle of life. Biological parents love their children from their core; it's a given.

Why is understanding this important? Because this blood bond between parent and child results in a natural trust by one parent in the goodwill of the other parent toward the child. When biological parents disagree, rarely if ever do you find them accusing each other of not loving the child. You don't hear one parent judging the other by saying, "You raised your voice to Kristin because you don't love her." No, the assumption is always that the other parent loves the child and has good intentions for the child's benefit.

This dynamic works differently in stepfamilies. It is very easy for a biological parent to question the motive of a stepparent. That's because the bond between stepparents and stepchildren is different—it isn't automatic. The relationship develops over time.

Strongly guard yourself against a harsh judgment of your wife's motives. You may not agree with her expectations or how she handles a situation, but be careful not to assume that she doesn't care about them. That accusation sets your heart against hers.

It is our experience that the vast majority of stepmothers have tremendous goodwill toward their stepchildren. Sometimes they do not feel the same love for stepchildren as they do their own children, and that's perfectly natural. However, it doesn't mean your wife isn't lovingly trying to do what is best for your kids. In a sense, her bond with your children can never equal yours, but her goodwill can.

Joanne kept complaining that Rob's kids didn't contribute to mowing the lawn or taking care of daily tasks in the home. Rob agreed they should do more, but when it came time for follow-through, he was a no-show. Joanne continued to complain. "Why can't you let this go?" Rob countered. "There are more important things in the world to worry about." In talking with their counselor, Rob finally discovered that his resistance was rooted in a lack of trust in Joanne's heart. He perceived Joanne as coldhearted and picking on his kids when, in fact, she was trying to equip them for independent living. Before Rob could hear her point of view and objectively consider it, he first had to trust her motives toward his kids.

> ### If Your Children's Mother Is Deceased
>
> You may find that it is a little more difficult to make room for shared parenting with your wife if your children's biological mother is deceased. After her death, the mantle of caretaking became your sole responsibility. Making space at this point might feel like letting go. Guilt will certainly be close by. Wrestle with your feelings and realize that allowing someone else to share the load of parenting does not mean you are neglecting or abandoning your children. It's a new season of life; embrace it.

Make Room for Shared Parenting. Matt was the only parent his children knew for several years. Even before their divorce, his ex-wife abandoned her role as mother. He lived a good distance from extended family; therefore, Matt was totally responsible for his children. Making space for his new bride, Paula, to join the parenting process was extremely difficult for him. He had never consulted anyone about parenting decisions. On one occasion Matt's teenage son asked for permission to go to a movie. Paula tried to interrupt the conversation in order to ask Matt to discuss this privately with her before giving his son an answer. But Matt made a quick decision, as he had done for years, and told his son he could go. In the process Paula's feelings were wounded, but he wasn't sure why. She explained, "It's like I don't matter at all."

It is understandable that Matt struggled to make room for Paula, but when he chose to remarry he needed to learn how to incorporate Paula into the parenting process. Doing so includes letting go of total control of his kids (which doesn't seem difficult until your wife has a different opinion from yours) and delaying decision-making until they could discuss the situation. It would also mean helping his children to get used to the change.

If Matt's children are like most, they will think it strange, at best, when their dad begins to take the time to talk through decisions with Paula. At worst, they will be very annoyed by it, especially if they are disappointed with the decision. Some measure of conflict and hurt feelings is predictable at this point. Paula will likely get the blame, and Matt will have to deal with his children when they complain or fuss about how things are changing. When his sixteen-year-old son objected to Paula's voice in decisions, Matt eventually learned to say things like, "Jared, I can see how difficult this is for you. Before I married Paula I made all the decisions and we went on with life. Paula is now my wife, so I'm going to include her as much as possible. I realize this is hard for you to understand because she's not your mother. I'm aware that some rules have changed and you can't do some things that you used to do, and naturally you don't like that. However, as your father I get to change my mind about some things and do what I think is best. We may have done things differently in the past, but this is how we're going to do things now. I don't expect you to be happy about every decision, but I do expect you to respect the decisions we make. We're doing what we think is best for you. I love you. And no, you can't stay out till 2:00 AM this Friday."

Getting the approval of the kids is not the goal, but rather developing a shared system of parenting, where you support the input of your wife. Making the shift will be a gradual process; stick with it and prayerfully endure the emotional hiccups.

Principle 3: Take the Primary Parenting Role With Your Kids

Making space for your wife's participation as an active member of the parenting team is important to her role as stepmother. In addition, your willingness to take the primary role in dealing with your children, especially around matters of nurturance and punishment, is crucial for the stepfamily. The story you just read about Matt and his son Jared is a good example. Taking the primary or "bad guy" role is not always fun, but it is necessary. Until your wife has developed a strong bond with your children, which can take many years, she can't take on that responsibility. It must fall to you. You have to be an engaged father.

The Engaged Father. An active, engaged father understands that the woman he married can be a wife much sooner than she can be a mother. Being a mother means she has established emotional trust and respect with the children to the degree that they elevate her to a place of authority.[2] This is a time-consuming, complicated process that is moderated by several issues, including the ages and personalities of your children, the relationship they have with their biological mother, the number of losses they have experienced, how much time they spend in your home—the list goes on and on. In other words, you are the safest, most well-defined parent figure in the home.

In his excellent manual on fathering, *The 7 Secrets of Effective Fathers,* Dr. Ken Canfield describes the qualities of extraordinary dads. According to Dr. Canfield's research, engaged fathers are committed to their children. They spend more time with their children than ordinary fathers, think about how to nurture their children, and are committed to maintaining their influence in the children's lives over time. They also know their children's needs, temperaments, and daily activities. They strive to be involved with their children in many contexts, like school, home, and in the community. They know something about child development (what to expect from children at given ages) and how their children compare to their peers. This knowledge helps them engage the children in appropriate ways. Other qualities include:

- responding consistently to the children over time in mood, morality, ethics, and interests
- protecting children by taking leadership within the home (especially at a time of crisis)
- providing a steady, reliable income for material needs
- providing children with a healthy model for masculine behavior toward a woman
- having good communication skills
- providing spiritual direction in the home.

This list may seem a bit overwhelming, but think of it as a road map for your role within your home. Growing in each of these areas can bring many blessings to your children over time.

The Disengaged Father. There are some fathers who completely disconnect from their kids because they don't care or are too selfish to invest in their children's lives. However, most dads who fall into the disengaged category didn't arrive there due to a lack of desire.

Step Money

"How can I feel like his partner when he insists that we maintain separate bank accounts?" Sometimes two (or three) accounts are a practical solution for couples and are not reflective of their relationship. But if this system creates insecurity in your marriage, revisit your rationale, restate your money values, and above all make sure your financial arrangements communicate commitment and permanence to each other.

One reason dads may disengage is because they are puzzled by child rearing and development and just aren't sure what to do. They love their children immensely but aren't equipped with discipline strategies and practical tools for parenting. These fathers would benefit from taking a class or reading quality books on parenting because good information can go a long way.

Other disengaged fathers are paralyzed by emotional exhaustion, fear, or guilt. The fear of losing the children to the former wife and guilt over what the kids have suffered can make a dad soft as a parent.

We sympathize with these overwhelming emotions. But the belief that taking it easy on the kids will somehow heal their pain simply isn't true. In fact, it prolongs it. They learn that being sad, depressed, or angry has benefits and "gets me what I want." Why change? They also learn maladaptive behavioral patterns, such as passive aggression, in order to cope with their stress. "Fine! I'll just go live at mom's house" carries a lot of weight with a guilt-paralyzed parent. It also sabotages any role the stepmother may attempt because she can't raise the standard for conduct any higher than you do. Empathy and sorrow for your children are normal emotions, but leniency shouldn't be the result. Guilt is not the problem. Being paralyzed by it is. If this describes how you've been parenting, admit it. Talk with your wife about how you might make changes and start leading now.

Smart Dating

During casual dating, it is probably best for the potential stepmom to have a hands-off posture. Once engaged you can intentionally begin to pass power to your fiancée and elevate her status in the minds of your children.

Keep in mind that her status will not be entirely tested until after the wedding. Only when she begins to enforce real-life consequences will you discover how much status the children are granting her.

Principle 4: Understand Her Level of Authority

During the past two decades stepfamily research has consistently shown that stepparents do not walk into the new family with the same amount of parenting power as biological parents.

Children have a variety of authority figures in their lives, and each person has his or her own level of influence or authority status. Teachers have authority over children, but not as much as parents. Coaches, camp counselors, and youth pastors all have a certain measure of power as well, but not as much as Grandma. Children accept authority from many sources.

The pace at which your wife progresses through each level is determined by numerous factors, such as the age of your child, previous family experiences (positive or negative), and whether the biological mother chastises your child for liking your wife.[3] The tempo is also impacted by the similarities between your parenting style and your wife's, plus how much you, as the dad, esteem and support her place in the family. Here are the differing levels of stepmom authority.

Level 1: Baby-sitter. Baby-sitters, like teachers, initially don't posses a great deal of status. In fact, they only have influence (or power) with children because the parent passes power to them. Children who are taught to respect all adults and various authorities in their lives during the first family and single-parent years have an easier time granting this level of status to stepmoms. For these kids, their stepmom is one more authority figure in their life that Dad expects them to obey. However, children who were not taught basic respect for adults early on may find it difficult to grant a stepmom even a low-level status.

> ## When Your Children's Mother Is Deceased
>
> A number of unique challenges can be experienced when your child's biological mother is deceased:
>
> - Each increase in status may resurrect grief in the child's heart. Allowing a stepmom more room in their heart may feel like "forgetting" Mom.
>
> - Children can unfairly compare how a stepmom parents to how they imagine their mother parenting them in this situation. Don't argue, but instead share, "That might have been your mom's rule/way of responding, but your stepmom and I have discussed this, and this is the rule now. I know you miss your mom and these changes probably remind you how much you miss her, right? [Shift the discussion to the child's sadness. Then conclude...] I know you wish things could be the same, but this is what we have to do now."

All stepparents start at level one. How long a stepmom remains at that level depends on a variety of dynamics that she often can't control. Baby-sitters only have as much power as the biological parent allows. Baby-sitters can enforce rules, expectations, and consequences, but they ultimately live on borrowed power from the biological parent.

Level 2: Aunt. Extended family members such as grandparents, aunts, or uncles typically have more authority with children than nonfamily members. Children naturally accept them as family and grant them a stronger voice of influence.

Stepmoms who grow into level two have relational authority that baby-sitter stepmoms do not. They are viewed as an extended family member and afforded a stronger influence. For example, in addition to enforcing household rules, it's possible your wife will make her own and find them respected. In stressful times, she'll need to fall back on your power and let you take the lead when imposing significant consequences.

Level 3: Parent Mentor. Some stepmoms achieve a high degree of influence and a healthy bond with stepchildren by taking on the role of parent mentor. When reaching adulthood, these children often refer to their stepmom as "the woman who raised me" or "one of my two moms." Emotional attachments are very strong and parental status high. These stepmothers don't blink when disciplining the children because the relationship has risen to a level of trust where the child doesn't question her authority.

When You Have Adult Children

Obviously, passing power to a stepmother of adult children is not critical to her role. She isn't trying to discipline them; she is trying to develop an adult-adult relationship or friendship. However, fathers should still communicate to adult children the expectation that they honor their stepmother as a significant part of his life. For example, inviting you to lunch but never inviting her does not show honor. Discuss with your children how family traditions and special family days will change because of her presence (which understandably may cause them irritation), and ask them to accommodate these changes out of respect for you.

There is no way to predict how long it will take for your wife to move from one level to another—or if an advance is possible. Therefore, refrain from making the next level a goal. Work as a team and learn to make wise choices whatever her present level.

Principle 5: Develop Common Ground in Parenting

A tremendous number of the couples I (Ron) work with in my counseling practice have a fundamental problem: They don't agree on how to raise the children. Even though they share the same mission (i.e., raising individuals who act justly, love mercy, and walk humbly with God), they disagree on how to accomplish the mission. You cannot assume that because you love each other your philosophies of parenting will fall in line. It takes communication and hard work to succeed.

In *The Remarriage Checkup*, I (Ron) and Dr. David Olson report findings from our national survey of couples in stepfamilies. We set out to discover the qualities of highly satisfied couples and what sets them apart from dissatisfied couples. Our results relative to parenting presented a clear contrast. Happy, satisfied couples were twice as likely as unhappy couples to have agreed on how to parent their

Smart Dating

Research on couples forming stepfamilies reveals:

- 86% of all couples have at least one partner who believes the children will put an additional strain on their marriage—and they're right!

- 25% of couples realize that their children do not have a positive attitude toward their marriage.

- 20% of all couples have concerns about the kind of parent or stepparent their partner will be; unhappy couples are six times more likely to have this concern than couples in strong relationships.

- Even while nearing the altar, nearly half of all couples have not yet agreed on how to discipline their children and stepchildren, and 40% have not discussed how to spiritually train their children.

- Couple dissatisfaction because of parenting issues increases after the wedding.

Most couples assume that relationships with stepchildren will improve after the wedding when, in fact, they usually get worse before getting better. Do not take for granted that your philosophies of parenting will work themselves out. Proactively discuss these matters before the wedding and don't get married unless you both feel confident in your plan.[4]

children. Also, two-thirds of unhappy, struggling couples did not agree on how to discipline their children. If you aren't sure what's the best way to respond in a given situation or you can't resolve an impasse, consult a minister, counselor, or mentor. Read a parenting book that offers objective advice or attend a class or seminar, but don't assume it will all work out. Actively pursing unity is the way to find a solution.

TEAMWORK: UNITED YOU STAND, DIVIDED YOU FALL

Everyone knows parenting works better when the adults are united in their approach and their position with the children. Finding this level of unity is harder in stepfamilies because both people didn't start from the beginning. The children came first, not your unified posture as leaders of the home. Therefore, both spouses must work at unity with great intentionality.

COUPLE PRAYER

After reading the chapter we encourage couples to pray this prayer together.

Heavenly Father,

You promise never to leave us or forsake us.[5] We stand today—as a couple trying to unite so we can lead this family—on that promise. Give us wisdom as we seek to work together in parenting; give us strength to face challenges that would divide us. Meld our hearts together.

We pray for our children that they might recognize the authority of their stepparent and not fear disloyalty or experience guilt. May they feel safety in the care of their stepmom.

Father, give us a trust in each other that surpasses blood bonds. Help us to act on the well-being of our children with the goal of teaching them responsibility, respect, and an appreciation of all that you have provided for them. May our parenting be a reflection of your parenting and your love for us.

We pray in Jesus' name. Amen.

Questions for Couples

Discuss these as you apply the information in this chapter.

1. On a scale from 1 to 10, rate your teamwork as parents. Share current strengths plus one thing you'd like to do better.

2. If the children were asked whether or not they feel their dad has fully declared his loyalty to his wife (the stepmom), what would they say?

3. Dad, how would you describe your wife's heart toward your children? When are the times you find it difficult to accept her opinion or involvement in parenting?

4. Dad, to what degree are you an engaged or a disengaged parent? When does guilt or fear paralyze you? What do you think it will take to improve?

5. Stepmom, does your husband stand with you on issues regarding his children? Give a specific example of a time when he backed you up, and then one when he didn't.

6. Dad, how do you regularly show appreciation to your wife for her role in your family?

7. For both: What is the most strategic thing you learned from this chapter?

8. For both: What is one area you need to change immediately?

Smart Stepmom Discussion Questions

1. What was the parenting style in your home growing up? Do you think this affects how you parent?

2. How has your husband's parenting style affected your marriage?

3. Do you have areas of concern for your husband as he parents his children?

4. Do you feel like a parenting team?

5. If your husband is an engaged father, how can you affirm this quality in him? If he is disengaged, showing respect may be a tremendous challenge. How might you continue to show respect while communicating your desire that he take a more active role?

6. What are your greatest concerns regarding your stepchildren and their future?

7. Is anything stopping you from lovingly sharing with your spouse how you really feel about his parenting style? What methods have you tried previously?

8. What have you learned from this chapter about healthy ways you could help your husband parent his children?

9. Are there ways your spouse acknowledges your efforts toward his kids?

10. Sometimes men need help understanding what a wife needs. What are specific things you could suggest to him that would help you to feel more appreciated?

Chapter 8

Dad Smart (Part 2): Pitfalls and Good Intentions

I thought that keeping peace with my ex-wife would reduce the stress for all of us. It didn't. In fact, it made things worse. I've learned that placating my former wife just made my present wife feel unimportant.

Jeff, remarried four years

A quick way to lose your wife's respect is to become passive with issues surrounding your children, ex-spouse, or extended family. Even well-intentioned, good-hearted fathers like Jeff can fall prey to a number of pitfalls. This chapter identifies the common pitfalls to avoid. You may have already fallen into a few of them. Don't beat yourself up—just climb out.

PITFALL 1: NOT UNDERSTANDING EMOTIONAL ATTACHMENTS IN CHILDREN

Piglet sidled up to Pooh from behind. "Pooh!" he whispered. "Yes, Piglet?"

"Nothing," said Piglet, taking Pooh's paw. "I just wanted to be sure of you."

A. A. Milne, Winnie the Pooh

We all have a God-given need to "sidle up" to someone and know they are there for us. Emotional attachments, as they are referred to, bring a sense of security, safety, protection, and love to our experience of ourselves and others. In the last thirty years researchers have learned a lot about children and their emotional attachments. For example, it's understood that secure attachment to key parental figures gives children a secure home base from which they can venture out into the world, knowing they always have a home to which they can return.[1]

Biological parents are the primary attachment figures for children. A strong bond with the child empowers the parents' ability to discipline, punish, and influence the child. This bond allows the child to grow emotionally and psychologically, explore his or her developing identity as it relates to the world, take chances with new relationships, and make choices about life values and spiritual beliefs. But a weak parental attachment short-circuits all of these processes. A child who has a close secure bond with one parent but an unreachable, unreliable bond with the parent in the other home will show signs of distress. Not unlike a baby who cries until they are held (which proves to the child that they can count on someone being there for them), children of all ages who don't have strong emotional attachments demonstrate their distress through protest (anger or complaining), clinging behavior (possessiveness and jealousy), depression (disengagment, self-criticism), and ultimately detachment (e.g., not wanting to spend time with a parent who has repeatedly rejected them). These distress reactions essentially scream, "Are you there for me?" Like Piglet, our children need to be sure of us.

Traumatic life experiences like parental divorce or the death of a parent result in attachment injuries that shake the foundation of a child's emotional stability. In chapter 4 we explain in depth how loss affects a child. Dad, your child has a need for security. His or her comfort comes from an emotional attachment with you, which is why it's vitally important for a biological parent to stay actively involved in the child's life. Through every life transition—including your remarriage—your child needs to be sure of you. Recognizing how attachment bonds vary with stepparents should also help you understand why your children may respond differently to your wife.

When Mom Is Deceased

A child's emotional attachment to a deceased parent continues after her death. Children should be encouraged to keep alive their thoughts and feelings toward their deceased parent. Talk with them about how they can make room in their heart for their stepmom while also keeping alive their mother's memory. God provides more than enough love in each of us for all the special people in our lives.

The Child Attachments chart summarizes some of the ways that you and your wife's emotional attachments with the children will impact their responsiveness. The essential difference is this: As the biological parent, you automatically possess a level of trust, love, and grace from your children that your wife must earn over time.

You are essential to your child; therefore, your child's default posture, even if they are furious with you, is one that preserves the relationship at all costs, extending grace. A child will seek out a parent's approval and love in countless ways (e.g., obedience, offering forgiveness, seeking attention). On the other hand, your child's relationship with your wife is confusing, at best questioning, "Do I even want you there for me?" and at worst costly: "Will loving you cost me the connection with my biological mom or others?" A common response to this confusion is for the child to act out with disobedience, anger, rejection, and accusations. What's a loving dad to do?

- *Acknowledge that attachments within your home may vary* (the chart offers descriptions). The bonding between your children and your wife may change over time—with either more or less

Child Attachments	
With Biological Parents	**With Stepparents**
Quick to offer grace in conflict. Children have a high tolerance for conflict and disappointment.	Low tolerance for conflict, easily angered and offended, capable of turning against.
"Insider" status. Children view parent as "part of the club" with all the rights and privileges of membership.	"Outsider" status. Viewed with a "you don't belong" attitude and a "you-have-to-earn-the-right-to-membership" status. If an insider (sibling, biological parent, extended family member) has a conflict with the stepparent, the insider will likely be supported and judged "right."
Auto-love. Love for the biological parent isn't decided, it's automatic and deeply felt.	Decision-love. Love must be created, nurtured, developed over time, and ultimately decided.
Auto-approval. This attitude says, "If Dad says it, it must be right," and results in a natural bias toward you. It gives the benefit of the doubt and seeks to justify why you are worthy of love (even if acting immorally or irresponsibly).	Decision-approval. Evaluates the stepparent to determine if they are worthy of approval. Is capable of rejection when in doubt.
Auto-trust. It is assumed that you can be trusted (even when proven otherwise).	Decision-trust. Trust is developed over time after the stepparent proves they have goodwill toward the child.
"My space is your space." This attitude says, "What's mine is yours; you have permission to enter my personal space."	"My space is mine." This attitude says, "Stepping into my space is a violation."

closeness. Hope and pray for the relationship to deepen, but don't assume you can cause it to happen quickly.

- *Younger children will likely attach more quickly than older ones.* Don't despair when the pace is different.

- *Listen to your wife.* Remember she doesn't experience your kids the same way that you do. You can't make everything okay for her, but you can listen with empathy. The deepest longing for most stepmoms is to have a husband who listens and believes when she speaks.

- *Require and maintain a standard of courteous behavior from your children toward your wife.* Even if they don't display deep affection for her, they should be courteous and respectful.

- *Encourage your children to forgive and show grace to your wife.* It may come at a slower pace than how they respond to you, but support it anyway. Home should be a place where all people are treated with grace.

- *Recognize that your emotional attachment to your children puts blinders on you.* Many stepmoms complain that their husbands, for example, view their little girl as a princess, without fault. When the father is away the stepmother witnesses the child's "true colors." Try to be objective about your child's behavior; taking off your blinders will not hurt your child and will facilitate teamwork with your wife.

PITFALL 2: AVOIDING THE MIRROR

Wise parents know how to look in the mirror. Men who desire to be excellent role models for their kids don't look merely at the children but at themselves. They are willing to examine their own motives, emotions, and beliefs about parenting. In addition, they examine how they interact with their wives and others who contribute to the parenting process (grandparents, ex-spouse, etc.).

Brian is a peacemaker. He grew up in a family where his father, also a peacemaker, accommodated his mother's preferences at every turn. "Going along," as his father would call it, kept conflict at bay in the home. Growing up, Brian followed his father's lead and was a very accommodating, well-behaved boy. This relationship pattern was so ingrained in Brian that he continued it into his first marriage.

This "no boundaries" style of relating appears to keep peace and win approval from others. But in the end it leads to the death of most relationships. After his divorce, Brian didn't look into the mirror and discover the root cause of the relationship failure; he continued catering to the preferences of his ex-wife. He adjusted his life to fit her schedule, and she dictated the visitation schedule. He even abided by her parenting rules at his house. Brian justified his behavior as doing the right thing for his kids. "It keeps our conflict down," he explained. "I don't want my children getting caught in the middle." We certainly advocate between-home cooperation after a divorce, which often translates into honoring the rules and preferences in both homes. But Brian's interaction is more about his inability to say no than dealing with co-parenting matters. He is stuck in a destructive, repetitive pattern that dictates his choices and paralyzes his relationships.

Oddly enough, because he is used to accommodating others, this pattern doesn't cause Brian emotional distress. While he was separated, his friends tried to tell him he was a pushover, but he ignored them. Then he got remarried to another assertive woman. Jody, a motivated career woman, loves the way Brian dotes on her. She is more than happy to speak her mind with Brian, and he accommodates her requests.

Both Jody and Brian describe their marriage as great; however, Jody does have one problem. "Brian won't ever tell his ex-wife no," she complains. "She signs the kids up for activities and then expects us to get them there on time. He refuses to tell her this is a problem. Now I am forced into going along too. He is a total wimp when it comes to his former wife, and I don't like it."

Brian has good intentions, but if he would look deeper he would recognize that he is more concerned about avoiding conflict than building healthy relationships. His fear of anger or disapproval from others is paralyzing his ability to parent properly or build a healthy relationship. When there was only one woman to keep happy (his ex-wife), things were manageable. But with two women pulling in opposite directions, Brian found it impossible to remain conflict-free.

A humble heart is open to self-examination and desires to let God's Spirit reveal truth. If you have a repetitive pattern that needs healing, the Lord knows how to heal it. Reach out for professional help or attend a support group geared toward overcoming these issues.

PITFALL 3: ALWAYS PLAYING DEFENSE

Feelings of guilt and fear cause some fathers to become paralyzed and others to defend their children. If someone were to ask your wife, "Are you able to approach your husband with concerns and discipline suggestions about his children?" how would she respond? Is defensiveness your first response to constructive suggestions, or are you willing to listen objectively?

Getting caught in the defensive trap is easy, in particular when you feel sorry for your children. You may feel they have been cheated out of a happy home. Laura's husband often shares that his heart grieves over the fact that his children did not grow up in the same type of intact, two-parent home that he himself enjoyed. This remorse can ignite a strong protectiveness against further hurt. However, if you are always defensive you will miss out on the opportunity to grow and improve your parenting, and your children will suffer.

PITFALL 4: IGNORING THE PARENTAL UNITY RULES

Did you know there are rules for maintaining parental unity? These rules create a positive process of working together.

- *Rule #1: Be proactive.* Don't wait until problems occur. Whenever possible anticipate situations and set boundaries. This should include behavior expectations, preferred methods of punishment and consequences to be enforced, and the values you wish to instill in the children.

- *Rule #2: When in doubt, call a parental powwow.* At my house (Ron), our children will occasionally hear the words "I don't know. I'll get back to you on that." My wife and I then have what we call a powwow or meeting to discuss our decision on how to handle a situation. This may be difficult if you have functioned quite well as a single dad and view yourself as a capable decision-maker. Do not underestimate the message this response is communicating to the kids. When your children recognize that you seek, respect, and honor your wife's input in parenting decisions, it will speak volumes about your unity as a couple. This will help to dissolve their efforts to "divide and conquer" the marriage. Even if it's inconvenient or uncomfortable, go the extra mile to ensure a parenting agreement. You won't regret it.

> ### Step Money
>
> Budgeting does not mean you can't purchase items you really want. Rather, it is a way of actively deciding what you will do with your money. As one wise person said, it is a way of telling money where you want it to go instead of wondering where it went. Developing and living within a budget can keep you out of financial trouble as well as decrease stress in your relationship.

- *Rule #3: If you don't appreciate how your wife handled a situation, have a private discussion.* The biggest mistake a father can make is to make negative, critical comments about the stepmom in front of the kids. The second biggest mistake is to reverse the decision behind your wife's back. Either of those responses robs her authority, which is already under scrutiny. The appropriate response is to listen to her explanation (kids often leave out significant details). If you don't agree with her decision, acknowledge her good intentions: "I appreciate that you were trying to teach Rebecca a lesson. I understand what you were attempting to accomplish." Then calmly share your thoughts about the situation and how you wish to handle it the next time. Refrain from turning this into a competition. The goal should be to find a solution that you can both support.

- *Rule #4: Communicate any major changes, new rules, or different expectations to the children together.* If you as a couple have decided on a rule change, it's best if Dad takes the lead in sharing the change with your wife standing beside you. This is particularly important in the early years of your remarriage. She can certainly add to the conversation, but your voice should clearly communicate unity in the transformation.

PITFALL 5: COWERING TO YOUR EX-WIFE

My husband will not ask his ex-wife to do the typical things a mother would do, like taking the kids to soccer practice. He refuses to ask her, so it gets dumped on us and we scramble to make it work. I'm not sure who he's married to—her or me.

Smart Dating

A word of caution to the dating, potential stepmom: In our experience, a failure by your boyfriend to manage pitfalls 3, 4, or 5 should be considered a significant red flag that you should not dismiss.

If before the wedding he is closed to your parenting observations or isn't working to include you in parenting decisions, you will likely experience even more distress after the wedding. And nothing can make your life more miserable than having a husband who cowers to his ex-wife.

Again, do not minimize these patterns. If you see them now, don't expect them to disappear after the wedding. We suggest you seriously consider delaying the marriage until you see significant changes.

For the man who is a "peaceaholic" such as Brian, one of the most difficult issues is standing between the former wife and the present wife. Many stepmoms feel this shouldn't be a difficult choice. But it's not that easy. Cowering to your former wife is typically about keeping peace for the sake of your kids. But doing so can create insecurity and frustration for your wife.

When the boundaries between you and your ex-wife weaken, or she gains power over your life and schedule, tension will instantly spike in your home and marriage. The key is to stand in that gap. The dad in the quote was attempting to keep peace with his ex-wife at the expense of resentment and insecurity in his home. Standing in the gap and setting a healthy boundary requires him to discuss a reasonable compromise with his former wife. She may balk or pitch a fit over the request, and he will need to explain what he will do if she doesn't comply. This could mean the child doesn't attend an activity arranged by the ex-wife (that she intended Dad to fulfill), plus she may speak badly about you behind your back. These are unfortunate circumstances that cannot be prevented. However, on behalf of your current marriage and home, it is still the best choice to make. If your former wife is used to controlling your life, it may take a few episodes before she realizes you are no longer a puppet on a string. Be prepared that she may try to turn the children against the stepmom, blaming her for the changes. Apologize to the children and share that you previously made the mistake of allowing their mom to dictate your schedule, but that you would have come to this conclusion even if you hadn't remarried.

Overcoming the fear of your ex-wife's wrath is essential to a healthy relationship.

PITFALL 6: MY KIDS AREN'T AS BAD AS YOURS

Gary had a trump card in his pocket. Each time his wife, Sonya, spoke negatively about his children or suggested he parent differently, he used his trump card against her. "You're one to talk. Your oldest son has made one bad choice after another—his life is in total shambles. And you want to tell *me* how to parent? What a joke."

Sonya's children were in their twenties and making bad choices. Gary used this as ammunition to discredit his wife's opinions of his children. This defense mechanism allowed him to diminish her influence.

When you discover that you are comparing your kids to your wife's as a way to dismiss their behavior or ignore your wife's opinion, there is a big problem brewing that needs to be addressed immediately.

PITFALL 7: A LOW STANDARD OF CONDUCT

Don't have a low standard of conduct for your kids. For example, if your wife expects her children to clean the kitchen after a meal but you let your kids leave a mess behind for others to clean, this creates distress. Work together to have an equitable standard of conduct for everyone.

PITFALL 8: ALLOWING DISRESPECT

When You Have Adult Stepchildren

Some fathers find that it is surprisingly more difficult to stand up for their wife's honor with adult children. Because you aren't in an active parenting mode with them, it can be awkward to assert your desire for them to honor your wife. Acknowledge their ongoing loyalty to their mother but ask them, if only out of respect for you, to graciously honor your wife at family occasions and events.

"Forsaking all others till death do us part." You likely said those words or something similar when you remarried. But, practically, what does it mean? We hope you've already learned that it does not mean neglecting your children. Your role in their lives is critical and cannot be replaced. However, your marriage vow does mean that your wife is to be honored at the highest level—and that you should encourage your children to honor her as your chosen bride. How does a dad do this? Take advantage of both the small and the significant moments in life.

One simple way of encouraging your children to honor your wife is by training your children (especially your son) to open doors for her. Another way to display honor toward her is to insist that your children use a respectful tone of voice. Addressing sarcasm or a sassy tone and insisting that they speak properly communicates her place of honor in the home.

Your wife needs an advocate, not an enemy. It's not about putting her on a pedestal or forcing others to see her as "number one," but more about elevating her status in your heart and theirs.

PITFALL 9: GUILT-TRIP MOTIVATION

"A real mother would not complain about taking Jacob back and forth to his activities. She would just be happy to do it." Randy was troubled when his wife, Sharon, expressed her frustration over all the time she spent doing things for his son. Laying a guilt trip on her was his method of coping. This stepmom was feeling taken for granted by Jacob and manipulated by Randy's ex-wife, who rarely found time to do her share of the taxi driving. Somehow Randy thought guilt would help the situation. Randy's underlying fear was that his wife's complaints were an indication that she didn't love his son. In an effort to urge her to move toward Jacob, Randy resorted to badgering laced with criticism. It didn't work because love never grows out of condemnation and guilt. His method seared Sharon's heart and increased her feelings of being unappreciated.

A wise dad learns not to be frightened or shocked by his wife's negative feelings toward his children. At times she may feel awkward, at other times angry, rejected, or jealous. You can't fix these feelings, so don't panic and try to make them instantly go away. Your job is to listen to her concerns, recognize the issue, and, if possible, walk toward a solution together. The fact that you are willing to hear her side and show a little compassion is typically what she is seeking.

CLIMBING OUT

After reading these common pitfalls you may see yourself at the bottom of a few of them. Don't lose heart. It's never too late to climb out. Begin by humbly acknowledging your circumstances and apologizing to your wife. The pit may not be entirely your fault; your wife may share in the responsibility as well. A soft heart of humility is always the first step to restoring solid ground.

Your wife's success as a stepmother depends heavily upon you. Without you, it's unlikely she will succeed. But with your support she can. We appreciate your taking the time to read these chapters with her. Our prayer is that they have united and encouraged you in how to be a better team.

COUPLE PRAYER

Pray this prayer together as a couple.

Heavenly Father,

We know your love for us is unconditional and runs very deep. We also know that our openness to you determines how close we are to you. Remind us that similarly our children and stepchildren will draw closer to us only when they are open. Help us to be patient with them when they are distant, and teach us to relish the close times. Give us the wisdom we need to love our children even when they do not act loving toward us.

So that we can be better parents, give us humility to look in the mirror and examine ourselves, noticing when we need to change. Remove our pride that is revealed in defensiveness and arguing so that we may make objective assessments of our children and their behavior. When punishment and discipline are required, give us the courage to act and follow through.

Above all, Lord, give us unity of spirit and the willingness to support each other in parenting. Let us be a solid parenting team that cannot be divided so that our children may learn to respect authority, and our marriage will stand the test of time.

Thank you for loving us even when we fall. And in your provision, thank you for this woman/man you have brought to partner with me in life.

In Jesus' name, amen.

Questions for Couples

Discuss these as you apply the information in this chapter.

1. Review the Child Attachments chart on page 143. Share some situations where you can see those dynamics at work. Discuss the implications for how each of you should relate to the children at this point in time.

2. When considering how you relate to each other and the children, what mirrors have been held up to you so far?

3. Dads: In the past when you've found yourself defending your children, what were you feeling? Try to uncover the fear, worry, or concern that pushed you to defend them. What needs to change for you to be set free?

4. Stepmoms: When have you seen your husband feeling caught between you and his ex-wife (or the memory of his deceased wife)?

5. Stepmoms: Share times that you feel honored in the marriage and home. When do you not feel honored?

6. Discuss any other matters that this chapter has brought to your attention.

7. Where do you feel this marriage is headed? Don't ignore the warning signs. If your marriage is in trouble, tell your spouse now! No matter how difficult or how unwilling your spouse is to hear your thoughts, honesty is crucial.

Smart Stepmom Discussion Questions

1. In what way does the Child Attachments chart bring relief to your heart? In what ways does it bring sadness?

2. Which of the pitfalls causes you the most distress?

3. In your opinion, what is the reason your husband might get caught in a pitfall? How can you show compassion for him while moving the family toward change?

4. What can you do to help your family move out of a pitfall?

5. Does your husband try to keep peace at all costs? If so, how can you lovingly help him to see this as a destructive choice? Are there resources or classes you could attend to address this issue?

6. Do you feel your husband honors you? If not, what are some ways you can calmly and logically explain this to him?

7. What did you learn from this chapter about how you can come alongside your husband in his parenting?

8. How has reading from a male perspective helped you to understand the complexities that surround your husband's situation?

Chapter 9

Meet Your Ex-Wife-in-Law: Friend or Foe?

"I just had no idea his former wife would be so involved in our lives," the new stepmom cried. "My husband is afraid of losing his visitation time, so he allows her to dictate our schedule. I feel like his former wife is the other woman in our marriage."

If your husband has an ex-wife, then you have what we have already referred to as an ex-wife-in-law. There is a significant reason we use the *in-law* term. Every person in your husband's extended family, including his ex-wife (or if they were never married, the mother of his children) and her new spouse (if she has one), is a member of your stepfamily. Similar to the in-laws acquired at marriage, his former wife is now a part of your family whether you like it or not.

One stepmom commented, "I don't

When Mom Is Deceased

A deceased mother is still a member of your family; therefore this chapter still applies to you. Her memory is part of the family story and very important to your husband and children. She has a presence in your home. This chapter can help you to explore the character traits of your deceased-wife-in-law and how her memory might impact your family.

want that woman to have any presence in my home." Fighting her presence is a natural desire, but the reality of divorce is that his former wife does have a presence in your home. The longer you deny this fact, the more frustrated you will become. It's also more likely that his children will resent your resistance to their mom and strive to keep her presence alive and active.

These kinds of issues aren't new. If you've ever read the Old Testament you know that most of the families were stepfamilies! Mostly the result of multiple marriages instead of divorces that preceded remarriage, stepfamilies in the Bible had dynamics very similar to stepfamilies today. Sarah, for example, was Abraham's first wife and had been expecting a baby promised by God. When she got tired of waiting for her pregnancy, she took matters into her own hands (ever get tired of waiting on God and try to take matters into your own hands?). In Genesis 16 she came up with what to us would be a horrible option, but was a common practice in that day: She offered her maidservant, Hagar, to Abraham as his second wife so they could have the promised child through her. The plan went awry when Hagar became pregnant with her son, Ishmael, and started belittling Sarah. The situation left Sarah feeling insecure, jealous, and very angry. This ignited an ongoing rivalry between Sarah and Hagar that lasted for many years. Later, when Sarah did become pregnant and had a son named Isaac, the rivalry escalated and spread to the children. Competition, jealousy, favoritism, and insecurity described their stepfamily experience.[1]

A significant part of creating a successful stepfamily is understanding and accepting that your family is spread across at least two homes. Emotionally, physically, and psychologically your family includes every person connected to either home. This dynamic is the foremost reason why stepfamilies, like Abraham, Sarah, and Hagar's family, are more complicated than biological families. If you map the relationships of your multi-home family, it's common to find three to five adults parenting three or more children.

And each individual, directly or indirectly, has influence upon the others. Your ex-wife-in-law is certainly one of those people. Stepmoms who defy this dynamic—or worse, try to disassemble the emotional connections—are typically angry, frustrated, dissatisfied, and depressed. The natural female desire to be your husband's "one and only" can cause a stepmom to disregard or despise his former wife. Often stepmoms have an overwhelming need to manage their own household and family schedule without interference or influence from his former wife. However, in a stepfamily, this isn't feasible and leads to a dangerous stance and family tension.

We are not suggesting that a stepmom should have absolutely no control over her home or schedule. But denying or trying to eliminate the ex-wife's existence by demanding that she has no role in the family dynamic is unwise and unrealistic. You may never love or even like your husband's former wife, but it's vitally important to acknowledge and accept that she is, in effect, a member of your family. It's not uncommon for a stepmom to disapprove of her actions or parenting choices. However, a Smart Stepmom recognizes that the biological mom is a part of the picture and learns how to deal with her as lovingly and reasonably as possible. "The Serenity Prayer" by Reinhold Niebuhr becomes her mantra: "God grant me the serenity to accept the things I cannot change, courage to change the things I can, and wisdom to know the difference."

THE NO-THREAT MESSAGE

"My former wife was the one who wanted out of the marriage. So why would she be so negative toward my new wife?" Doug asked. "The kids are influenced by her vicious comments, and if she continues, my new wife, Tracy, doesn't stand a chance with them." Doug's question is not an easy one. There could be a host of reasons why his ex-wife would try to poison the children against Tracy. One common reason is fear. His ex-wife might feel threatened and jealous of

Tracy. One thing is certain: Her negative comments communicate to the kids that she wants their loyalty. Most likely they will easily comply because showing devotion to their biological mom temporarily soothes her fears. Children are almost always more loyal to a biological parent than they are to a stepparent. This mother doesn't need to manipulate the children by pulling their loyalty strings, but insecurity creates an anxiety that causes her to do so.

An important step a Smart Stepmom should take regarding the former wife is to communicate the No-Threat Message. This respectful and honoring communication speaks directly to the former wife's perceived threat. It is an attempt to reduce the fears of a former wife who is prone to injecting her kids with poison against the stepmom.

Verbal communication is best, but for the stepmom coping with a hostile environment or a moderate level of tension, the message can be communicated by email or letter.

> *Meghan, since we are both involved with your kids, I wanted to take a minute to communicate with you. I want to share that I totally understand and respect that you are the only mother of these children. I'm not their mom, and I will never try to take your place. They are your children. I am honored to be an added parent figure in their lives. I view my role as one of support to their father, and my desire is to be a blessing to them. I promise to speak well of you and work together for their benefit. I desire to make their lives easier, not more difficult. Please know that I pray for the entire family. If there's anything I can do to help the situation or if you have any questions, feel free to contact me.*

I (Laura) never knew to send a letter like this to my husband's former wife. However, I believe that my childhood experience and the stress of having a stepmom helped me to communicate the message without words. I've worked hard to make certain that my stepsons and their mother know I'm not vying for a mom position. I am not their mom—I am their dad's wife—and I don't expect them to view me in a mom role. Accepting this as reality and clearly communicating the message have prevented me from disappointment and conflict with my ex-wife-in-law.

Whenever possible I show honor and respect for and to the boys' mom. For example, when there was only one special seat available at a graduation, concert, or a special school event, I viewed that as her place, not mine. I haven't been perfect, but I strive to keep the kids from feeling torn between us.

Also take into consideration the reasons for your husband's divorce. If he abandoned his former family due to irresponsibility, addiction, abuse, or an adulterous affair, it's possible his ex-wife is still deeply hurting or angry. Those wounds could be the root cause of her inflammatory remarks directed toward you.

In any circumstance your goal needs to be to live out the No-Threat Message. Actions will substantiate the words that you have no desire to become a threat to the relationship the former wife has with her children. Over time she may grow to believe you. Hopefully this will result in fewer toxic words and a better relationship.

TYPES OF BIOLOGICAL MOMS

Not all ex-wives-in-law are the same. Recognizing his former wife's strengths and weaknesses can bring a helpful perspective to the task of shared parenting.

We have listed several types of biological moms. Your ex-wife-in-law may have the attributes of more than one category. Deceased mothers live on in the memories of their children and former husband; therefore, consider these categories if your husband was a widower. While you don't have the ability to interact with a deceased mother and assess her yourself, the stories that are told about her will tell you which type of mom she was and how she is remembered.

Adult Stepchildren

These descriptions can also apply to biological moms with grown children.

The Open Mom

This is the woman every stepmom longs for as an ex-wife-in-law. She is the lady who truly loves her kids and recognizes that working together as a multi-household team is what is best for the children. Not insecure, but confident in her place in her child's heart, she is open to your stepmom role and influence with her children. This kind of mom often finds her identity and strength in God, and she has forgiven her former husband for issues surrounding their divorce. She actually prays that you will be a positive role model for her kids and that they will get along with you and even love you.

One stepmom shared, "Even though the biological mom doesn't always use good judgment, she has a great heart and loves her kids. She communicates with me for the sake of the children. We have a good relationship, and we both go out of our way for the other."

Deceased "open moms" were gracious and welcoming of new people. This kind and compassionate spirit is often passed on to the surviving family members, who eventually find a way to let you in.

The Martha Stewart Mom

"I can't live up to the standards of the 'real' mom. I feel like I'm supposed to cook, clean, and even decorate like she does. But that's not my personality," states one stepmom.

Trying to emulate the former wife—living or deceased—is an unwise task. Don't let anyone pressure you into becoming something you are not. If making sandwiches or pizza rather than a big, home-cooked meal is normal for you, then so be it. Just because she bakes her own bread or makes homemade costumes for the Christmas pageant does not mean you must follow suit. Resist the urge to become supermom.

Learn the things you do well and implement those things into the lives of your stepkids. God doesn't expect you to change your personality or take on abilities you don't posses just because you became a stepmom.

The Protector Mom

When this biological mother remarries she feels the need to protect her children from her own new husband.[2] It's possible that she may try to guard her children from you as well. Some of this is a natural, God-given maternal instinct to protect a child. However, as we discussed earlier, her attempt to shield the kids may be caused by a fear that you will interfere with her role as Mother. She also might respond to you as a gatekeeper who carefully analyzes how you are influencing her children. This too is natural, especially if she perceives that you do not have their best interests at heart. If that's the case she may try to:

- limit your access to the children (e.g., change the visitation schedule)

- reduce your intellectual influence (e.g., argue your political views)

- sabotage your emotional connection with the children (e.g., make negative comments).

This mom will need to see and experience your goodwill toward her children, and the No-Threat Message is crucial for her.

The Overinvolved Mom

This mom gives the appearance of being a healthy, engaging mother to her children and an open mom to you. However, she is enmeshed with her children and cannot separate herself from their lives. Her entire identity comes from being a mom, which compels her to be the center of their emotional lives. This is not to be confused with a biological mom who has recently experienced a divorce and is naturally concerned about her children. The mom we are describing obsesses about her children, even years after the divorce, and may go to pieces when the children leave her presence or visit your home. An indication of this type of mom is that her insecurity causes her to stay in touch with her children continuously. For example, we know a father who provided cell phones to his children, but the mom tossed them and bought them new cell phones with unlimited text messaging. Then she made the kids promise to keep the phone numbers a secret from their father so he couldn't interrupt their communication. The overinvolved mom is tenacious and controlling. She appears to be cooperative in co-parenting matters; however, in reality she is passive-aggressive. Because this behavioral pattern is normal for her, your husband may not recognize her manipulation or he may go to the other extreme to ignore her tactics. This may force you to interact with her.

> ### Smart Dating
>
> A biological mom may not show her true colors until you are married. Even if she was the one who desired divorce, her former husband's remarriage to you can bring all of her emotions, regrets, anger, or pain to the surface. This woman may appear open or distant before your wedding, but she may shift into a more assertive role afterward.
>
> In order to alleviate unnecessary fear, begin communicating the No-Threat Message as soon as marriage seems certain.

In this situation, the No-Threat Message will likely fall on deaf ears because her fears and insecurity are immense. She needs to be needed by her children. It's her reason to breathe. Not all of the children will accommodate her smothering parenting style, but it's likely at least one child will (often a daughter). This will be your challenge child because warming up to you means betraying her mom—and most children can't do it even if they want to.

Step carefully with this mother. If you give her added cause to view you as an enemy, life will be extremely difficult.

The Stonewalling Mom

Before we were engaged, my husband tried to introduce me to his former wife. I didn't think it would be an issue because she was the one who wanted out of their marriage. We were in a public place and when we walked over to her, she turned and walked away. After four years she has still never spoken one word to me—ever. I've tried to show her that I have no desire to take her kids away. I know the kids feel the stress and tension when she drops them off. I don't understand it, but she absolutely refuses to acknowledge that I exist.

Pam

This stepmom is in a no-win situation. There is nothing you can do when the biological mom refuses to communicate or work with you in any way. In this situation the Smart Stepmom ministers to the kids the best way she can. If the children mention the other home or their mom, she is wise to listen but not criticize. If the children ask questions, her role is to answer them honestly but without condemnation of the biological mom. As the old saying goes, "Blood is thicker than water." A good response might be something such as, "Dustin, I'm sorry that the tension between your mom and me causes you to feel bad. I want you to know that I don't understand why she won't talk to me, but I don't wish her any harm either. She is your mom, and I know she loves you. Would you like to talk about how this tension makes you feel? Is there anything I can do to make it easier for you?"

One stepmom in a similar situation shared that when her stepkids saw that she was the one to pick them up for visitation and not their father, their expressions instantly changed from happiness to stress. As they transitioned from Mom's car to hers, the stress and tension they felt was enormous. On their behalf she insisted that in the future her husband would need to pick up the kids. She didn't do this to protect herself, but because she could see the pain his kids were experiencing.

If you are dealing with a stonewalling Mom, your only option is to pray for her, stand alongside your spouse, and draw as close to the kids as they will allow. And know that all the communication and logistics between homes will fall on your husband.

The Distant, Abusive, or Addicted Mom

This woman may have left your husband and her children for self-ish reasons or due to an addiction. It's possible that she has little or no contact with the children. This mom may periodically have a desire to be involved in their lives, but she is irresponsible and undependable. Her life and decisions are chaotic; instability is her middle name.

She is often preoccupied with her career, her newest dating relationship, or an addiction. She may be verbally, physically, or emotionally abusive, which means she is also spiritually abusive (wounds to the heart always wound the soul). In some situations, legal authorities can (and should) intervene to prevent extreme harm to the children. Perhaps their intervention will bring Mom a change of heart. Consult an attorney in your area (each state and region is managed differently) to fully understand the options and consequences. Make absolutely certain your motives are pure, pray for clarity, and act with resolve when necessary. However, even then her influence leaves a dark residue of shame and pain on the entire family.

Regardless of the circumstances, this mother presents a huge challenge to stepmoms. Her irresponsible and unpredictable behavior causes a constant threat to the stability of your home. Her children resent her one day and miss her the next. She repeatedly hurts the children, but the natural loyalty of kids keeps them pining for her return. Her ambiguity keeps everyone, including you, searching for solid ground. Surviving in this situation requires that the stepmom discover how to live with the not knowing. It also requires a tolerance for the vacillating emotions of closeness and distance often portrayed by the kids. Unfortunately, their openness to you is often a direct reflection of her movement in and out of their lives.

If you are dealing with a biological mom who has any of the

above destructive qualities, one big question arises: In what ways can we promote peace and not more chaos?

DEALING WITH A DESTRUCTIVE MOM

"It doesn't matter what we do; his ex-wife is unreasonable, bitter, and downright mean. We have tried everything you suggest and yet she continues. What are we supposed to do?" If this is your question, the good news is that God's Word offers guidelines to help you cope.

Legend has it that years ago, in a large southeastern city, the great pianist Paderewski was scheduled to perform. The city was alive with excitement when the day finally came. In the crowd at the concert was a young mother clutching the hand of her small son. Hoping to inspire him to practice, she had brought him to hear the master perform. As they sat and waited for the concert to begin, she turned her head to look at the people as they filled the auditorium. The little boy saw his chance to escape.

He quietly slipped from his seat, and walked down the aisle toward the stage. Just as he reached the orchestra pit, a spotlight hit the grand piano and he gasped at the beauty of the instrument. No one noticed the little boy as he slipped up the side stairs to the stage and climbed up on the piano stool. No one noticed him at all, until he began to play "Chopsticks." The concert hall fell silent.

Then people began to shout. "Get him away from that piano!" Backstage, the master heard the crowd; he grabbed his coat and rushed to the little boy's side. Without a word, he bent down and, placing his hands on either side of the boy's, began to compose a beautiful counter melody to "Chopsticks." As they played together, he whispered in the little boy's ear, "Don't stop! Keep on! Don't quit!"[3]

In the same way that this musical genius wrapped his arms around this little boy and encouraged him to "Keep on! Don't Quit!" your heavenly Master is doing the same thing for you, Smart Stepmom. On your own you most likely won't have the strength, determination, or passion to deal with a destructive biological mom or perhaps go the distance in this marriage. If you decide to go it alone without God's help, you might be able to squeak out a simple version of "Chopsticks." But imagine the music you can play if you allow yourself to be completely embraced and protected by the Holy One, the Creator. He longs to help you.

Psalm 40:1–3 gives instruction for coping with debilitating circumstances. In this Scripture we see a person in deep, dark trouble. There seems no way out of the pit. But God points the way to victory. The first step is to look beyond the circumstances, past the pit, and up to God: "I waited patiently for the Lord."

The second step is to cry out to God. Let him know how you feel. It's okay. Don't be afraid or embarrassed. God is big enough to handle your pain, fear, or frustration: "He turned to me and heard my cry."

The third step is to trust that God will show up and do what he does best—heal, redeem, and restore. "He lifted me out of the slimy pit, out of the mud and mire; he set my feet on a rock and gave me a firm place to stand." Notice that God lifts the person out of the pit; he or she doesn't get out on personal strength. This is extremely significant because our natural tendency is to think we are required to do this on our own ability, and nothing could be further from the truth. That is the reason why most people give up and fail.

And then, at last—victory. "He put a new song in my mouth, a hymn of praise to our God. Many will see and fear and put their trust in the Lord." Who is capable of placing a new song in the mouth? God gives the discouraged person a new song, a new perspective, a new hope! How? Let's keep walking.

When you accept Jesus Christ as your Savior, the Holy Spirit comes to dwell within you. Philippians 2:5 tells us that the Holy Spirit is willing and capable to give us the mind of Christ: "Let this mind be in you, which was also in Christ Jesus" (KJV). That means we now have the ability to think and act like Jesus. I can't speak for you, but for me (Laura), this is incredibly good news. Because left to my own thoughts and actions, I can be nasty—in particular if I'm being slandered, criticized, or ridiculed as a stepmom. But God's Word tells me there is a better way to respond, a method that can motivate peace rather than destruction.

The twelfth chapter of Romans encourages us with instruction. Verse one says, "In view of God's mercy . . . offer your bodies as living sacrifices, holy and pleasing to God." Verse eighteen goes on to add, "If it is possible, as far as it depends on you, live at peace with everyone." If you're like us, that sounds challenging but manageable, depending on the one you are trying to live at peace with. Sacrificing for a neighbor that you like, or giving of your time and money to care for the poor, feels noble. But being a living sacrifice for a difficult ex-wife-in-law may not sound inviting or feasible.

In his infinite wisdom, God gives us specific instructions in the latter section of Romans 12 on how to love someone we can't stand.[4] There Paul outlines the attitudes and actions of what it means to love difficult people.

First and foremost, the underlying problem we need to acknowledge is sin. Regardless of your ex-wife-in-law's motivation, if she is acting out in destructive behavior that is harming your home, the root cause is evil. God's prescription for overcoming evil is direct: "Overcome evil with good" (v. 21). The temptation we all face is to repay evil with more evil. But that is not in keeping with the mercies God has shown us in verse one of this chapter. Therefore the goal, in spite of the hurt we experience at the hands of others, is to offer ourselves as living sacrifices and repay evil with good. But what about revenge? Isn't that justified?

Vengeance is not inherently bad; it's just not ours to take. Romans 12:19 makes it clear that God is the only one who should seek vengeance. He is the only one who is pure and holy, with no ulterior motives. He always desires our higher good. If your husband's former wife chooses to continue with evil, destructive deeds instead of good, it is God's job to do what is best. Not yours.

But what is your role in the meantime? Are you supposed to sit around and passively wait for more persecution? No—you must become aggressive with good. When wicked behavior is running rampant, it feels like it's in control. But God's Word tells us that good is more powerful than evil. God does not say that doing good to others will help us tolerate their evil. He says that we can *overcome* it. Light overwhelms darkness. Hope triumphs over discouragement. Love casts out fear. It is our task, in the face of evil, to offer good. Why? Because good invites repentance. Consider Romans 12:20: "If your enemy is hungry, feed him; if he is thirsty, give him something to drink. In doing this, you will heap burning coals on his head." The phrase "heap burning coals on his head" referred to awakening the conscience of another. With good, we can melt the heart of evil with burning shame. Constantly repaying evil with good holds a mirror up to the perpetrator reflecting only their evil; in some cases this will bring about a change of heart.

As a counselor I (Ron) became curious when an ex-wife called to make an appointment at the encouragement of her former husband's new wife (the stepmother). I had worked with the stepmother, Patty, and her husband to improve some dynamics in their family. Now, a few months later, Patty's ex-wife-in-law, Carrie, was calling for an appointment regarding her recent remarriage. "I have come to trust Patty and her recommendations," Carrie said. "But it didn't start out that way. When she first married my ex-husband I thought she was the enemy, and I was threatened by her. But she has proven herself time and again to be decent and pure of heart. I actually consider her a friend at this point." There is such power in stubborn goodness.

But what if repentance does not happen in the heart of the destructive mom? Then it's between your ex-wife-in-law and her Creator. You may suffer much at her hand, but you must trust God to do what is right. And what do you get for your obedience? Another place in Scripture concludes that the Lord will reward those who do good to those who are evil (see Proverbs 25:21–22). The evil of some ex-wives-in-law can be overcome; others cannot. Either way, the Lord will notice your sacrifice and reward you.

Until then live this way (see Romans 12:14–20):

- bless and do not curse
- do everything you can to live in harmony
- do not be proud, and be willing to associate with her despite her behavior
- do not become conceited
- in public be careful to do what is right
- do not take revenge
- "feed her" and "give her something to drink," even when undeserved.

FORGIVENESS: WHAT IT IS—WHAT IT ISN'T

The final step to obtaining victory over anger and bitterness is to learn how to forgive, and the best way to step forward is to admit that you need help. Be honest with the Lord, no matter how angry you are. Ask him to reveal any distorted or unhealthy thinking you may have about forgiveness. God is more than willing to teach you how to surrender every hurt and rejection to him so that it produces wholeness. If you desire forgiveness for your own sins, the Bible states that you need to forgive others (Matthew 6:14–15). And that often begins with discovering the difference between what forgiveness is and what it is not.

The main reason so many people resist forgiving another person is because of a distorted definition of the word. We have clearly explained that loving as Christ would have us love requires surrendering to him and becoming a living sacrifice. However, in order to complete the process it's important to understand what forgiveness is and dispel what forgiveness is not.

Forgiveness is not a feeling.

If you are waiting until the feeling to forgive comes upon you, it's unlikely to occur. Forgiveness is an act of obedience to God because we trust him and believe he has our best interest at heart. When we cling to revenge, anger, and rage it often destroys us spiritually, emotionally, and physically. Christ paid too much for his beloved ones to become slaves to anything, much less hatred. He wants his children free. And a person is never free when he or she is weighed down with the ball and chain of bitterness. When the cold shackles of revenge are tightly clasped around our wrists, it's impossible to lift our hands in praise to him.

Forgiveness is not pretending you were not hurt.

Walking around with a painted-on smile when you are emotionally dying inside is not forgiveness. In Scripture we never see Jesus pretend. When he is sad, he weeps (John 11:35). When he is angry, he turns over the tables (John 2:15–16). When he is lonely, he cries to his daddy (Matthew 26:39). Christianity is not about denying a wound when someone has damaged your soul or inflicted pain into your life. You are justified to recognize and claim the hurt instigated by another's sinful or poor choices. It's when we use the pain as a weapon and retaliate with revenge that we disobey God.

Forgiveness is not saying what the person did is okay.

Many people reject forgiveness because it feels as though the wrongdoer is getting away with the offense. Our human nature wants the person who hurt us to suffer. Forgiveness isn't ignoring what the person did or pretending they are wonderful. It's giving the offense to the One who will judge righteously.

Forgiveness does not require trusting the person.

The majority of misunderstandings about forgiveness fall under this category. When a betrayal has occurred in a relationship with a loved one, it is crucial for trust to be restored over time if the relationship is to survive. However, forgiving your ex-wife-in-law is a different circumstance because you are not attempting to regain a friendship. In this circumstance it's perfectly okay to guard your heart. However, that doesn't eliminate your responsibility to respond to her in a Christlike manner.

Forgiveness does not relieve the person of responsibility.

Forgiveness doesn't eradicate responsibility, and it's not unloving to hold someone accountable. It's often the most loving thing you can do because it could lead to repentance. However, in situations regarding stepfamilies, it's often the dad who is required to hold his former wife responsible to her commitments. Your job as the stepmom is to support him.

Forgiveness is frequently not a one-time event.

If you are dealing with a difficult or wounded ex-wife-in-law, she may hurt you repeatedly. This will require asking God to teach you over and over again how to forgive. God often allows someone who is difficult into our lives so that we learn to depend on him rather than ourselves for strength.

SETTING BOUNDARIES

Understand that seeking harmony and responding to evil with good does not mean you must allow his former wife to physically or mentally abuse you. It also doesn't mean that your spouse should not stand up for and defend you when she attacks. A husband is supposed to protect his wife, even if it's from his former wife. In addition, loving as Christ doesn't mean you should put your life, your home, or your children in jeopardy. Ramira shares her situation.

> *My husband's former wife has addiction issues. She is on her third marriage, and her family and friends have all abandoned her. I sense she is reaching out to me for friendship. I give her food, furniture, and the things she needs. I encourage her over the phone, and I pray for her. I've passed on information about support groups that could help, but I'm afraid to bring her chaos into our home. We have small children, and she lives a dangerous life. I want to show her the love of Christ, and my heart aches for her, but I need to protect my family also.*

Ramira is a Smart Stepmom. She understands that she can't fix or change the biological mom; it's not her job. She is showing her the love and compassion of Christ, but that doesn't mean she needs to get caught up in the drama of her life. Sometimes knowing where to draw the line can be difficult. But if you seek God, he will show you when and how to help, and when to let go.

The complexities described in this chapter are some of the key reasons why it's vitally important for you to connect with other stepmoms. You need a support system. To learn how to create a network of stepmoms in your community or to find a Smart Stepmom workshop near you, search *www.thesmartstepmom.com*. In addition, the book *Sandpaper People: Dealing With the Ones Who Rub You the Wrong Way* by Mary Southerland is a great resource to help you deal with difficult people. And lastly, remember the words of Charles Spurgeon: "Anxiety does not empty tomorrow of its sorrow, but only empties today of its strength."

PRAYER

Dear Lord,

You have called me to a large task—complete surrender. I praise you that even the ability to have faith in you comes from you. I am weak but you are strong. I am not alone; you are with me.

Right now I don't like my husband's former wife, much less desire to show her kindness or compassion. I confess that there are times I wish she would move far away or disappear. I'm embarrassed to confess that there are times I hate her. Her words and actions wound me, Lord. She treats me with such contempt, and I don't know how to respond. But you do. Forgive me for detesting her. The desire of my heart is to honor you more than I desire to retaliate and hurt her.

I thank you that you do not ask me to climb out of this dark pit on my own, but that you are willing to lift me out and place my feet on solid—not shaky—ground. You are willing to transform my mind and teach me how to think as you do. I praise you for this supernatural gift. I praise you that you alone can teach me how to forgive my husband's ex-wife. Teach me how to live in harmony with this woman, Lord. Help me to see her through your merciful eyes and not my own. Help me to extend the same grace to her that you have shown me.

You alone are the desire of my heart. I want to obey you. I trust your words and your ways to bring peace into my life. Amen.

PRAYER REFERENCES

Psalm 40:2–3   *Matthew 6:14–15*
Romans 12

Smart Stepmom Discussion Questions

1. Why do you think it is important to accept your ex-wife-in-law (and her extended family) as part of your family?

2. Discuss the purpose of the No-Threat Message.

   • Which communication method is best for you (verbal, email, or letter)?

   • What actions can you take to live out this message?

3. Which type of biological mom best describes your ex-wife-in-law? What are the specific challenges you face while interacting with her?

4. Did you learn anything new about how to interact with your husband's former wife?

5. How do you respond to the story about Paderewski and the child? Do you have a relationship with God that allows him to embrace you?

6. Read Psalm 40:1–3 aloud. In what ways does this psalm relate to your situation? Do you have difficulty trusting God to lift you from the pit?

7. In what ways can you take the steps suggested to:

   • look beyond the circumstances, and up to God

   • cry out to your Creator

   • trust God to show up

8. Are you ready for God to put a new song in your mouth? What would that song sound like? Take a moment to write a few sentences in response to these insights:

_____

_____

_____

_____

_____

_____

_____

_____

9. Are you struggling to believe that you can overcome evil with good? What lessons did you glean from Romans 12 for coping with a destructive mom?

10. How has your view of forgiveness been affected or changed by reading this chapter?

11. In what ways do you struggle with setting boundaries concerning your ex-wife-in-law? How could you better communicate with your spouse about those issues?

12. In what ways has this information helped you to assist another stepmom who is struggling with her husband's former wife?

Chapter 10

Understanding Your Kids: What Do They Need?

"Ron, I feel so bad for my son. I just don't know how to help him."
Cara, a mom and stepmom, was referring to her fifteen-year-old
son, Jackson. During a counseling session Cara and her husband
explained that Jackson and his stepfather got along great. The problem for Jackson was his stepbrother. Cara shifted in her seat rather
anxiously and continued.

"When my stepson is disrespectful,
Jackson becomes furious. He tries to defend
me and stand up to his stepbrother, but that
just adds to the conflict. He hates how my
stepson treats me. And when Stephanie
[Cara's ex-wife-in-law] spreads rumors
about me or stirs up trouble, Jackson gets
mad. I don't know how to help him."

We know how much you care for your
children; becoming a stepmom doesn't
minimize the deep love you have for your

> ## No Children of Your Own?
>
> Even if you didn't bring chil-
> dren to this marriage, we rec-
> ommend you read this chapter.
> You will receive insight into
> the emotional dilemmas your
> husband faces while parent-
> ing his children. Balancing
> parental responsibilities and
> spousal commitments can be
> challenging. Read this chapter
> with an eye for how it applies
> to your home.

own. And yet the uncertainty of being a stepmother and the challenges of stepfamily living can present difficulties to your children and may complicate or minimize your time with them. You would be quite normal if you felt guilty and anxious on their behalf.

Your children don't have to get lost in the shuffle; we have some prescriptions to keep you connected. But first, there are some temptations to avoid.

TEMPTATIONS TO AVOID

Our first word of advice is to refrain from underestimating the emotional and psychological adjustment your children may have to a stepfamily. Getting a second chance at love may cause you to overlook the ways your children are struggling. In earlier chapters we discussed the losses and loyalty conflicts faced by your stepchildren; your children face these same issues as well.

Marsha sat with her jaw dropped in a counseling session. She was listening to their family therapist as he spoke with her children about all the transitions and adjustments they had faced since her remarriage. Moving to a new city and, therefore, a new school, house, and church were just the beginning. Their stepdad parented very differently from their mom, plus his children were hard to get to know. They felt confused much of the time and weren't sure what to make of all the changes. The more they talked, the more Marsha's eyes welled up with tears; she was hearing them for the first time. Marsha was grieved because she realized this marriage had brought further emotional and psychological uncertainty for her children. Yes, it also brought some blessings, but she was just beginning to realize the depth of their discomfort.

Throughout the formation of your family, it is extremely important to remain emotionally connected to your kids, to give them permission to express sadness, and to provide reassurance that they are loved and safe. This includes guidance through the awkwardness of bonding with new family members. Listening to the realities of their experience (and not trying to fix their pain) is an important first step. We'll share more nurturing strategies later in the chapter.

If love and romance leads some mothers to be blinded to their children's needs, guilt leads others to anxiously hover over their children. This produces a second temptation: remaining more committed to being a mom than being a wife. In chapter 7 we challenged your husband to declare to his children his undying loyalty to you; doing so communicates the permanence of your marriage and empowers you as a stepmom. It also builds security and confidence in your marriage. You must make that same pledge of loyalty to him.

The temptation to prioritize your children above your spouse may be fueled by worry. If their biological father is disengaged, undependable, or lacking in parental competence, or if they seem to be getting lost in the new family, you may get trapped protecting them at every turn. Finding the balance in caring for their needs and maintaining a strong commitment to your husband is a difficult challenge but a necessary one. Neither should be neglected. There may be seasons when you focus on a child or all of your children in order to help them through a difficulty, but refrain from losing sight of your marriage. Caring for your children is not a problem, but feeding your children and starving your marriage is.

This temptation to prioritize your children over your husband can also be driven by the fear that giving yourself entirely to your husband could result in heartache. This is particularly true if your first husband was abusive or he betrayed or abandoned you. I (Ron) refer to this as the risk-assessment approach to marriage. It results in the cancerous conclusion that children are a safer emotional bet than a husband because, as some women will say, marriages come and go but children are forever. Investing all of yourself in your husband *is* emotionally risky, but it is absolutely necessary if you wish for the marriage to last. If this feels like a contradiction to our first point, that your children shouldn't feel forgotten, remember we aren't saying that it's *either* your children *or* your husband. Instead, strive to love *both* your husband *and* your children while declaring a long-term dedication to your marriage.

It's possible that we just lost some of you. You may be struggling or angry because it appears that we are saying you should abandon your kids for the sake of your marriage. That's incorrect. Let us explain.

When couples in a first marriage have children, they broaden their primary relationship focus. Before children, they focus exclusively on each other; children are then incorporated into this primary love relationship, but they don't overshadow it. Throughout the child-rearing years healthy couples in first marriages devote countless hours to their children's activities and interests. And yet the children and adults both understand that the marriage is the core relationship in the family and that it will endure long after the children leave home. This dynamic is what we encourage you to establish in your stepfamily.

You should continue to spend a significant amount of time with your children, nurturing their spirits and shaping their characters. And yet it is imperative for your marriage to be established as the long-term foundation of your home. During your single-parent years, your role as a parent was the foundation of your home. But now that you have married, the foundation needs to be your marriage.

Notably, here's where stepfamilies become extremely complicated. Children in a biological family feel secure when their parents are happily married. Life is

Dating Single Parents

A word of caution: If you are not ready to make the transition of placing your marriage as the priority before your children, we strongly urge you to refrain from marriage until you are ready. Many stepmoms share, "I had no idea that getting married meant putting my new husband before my kids. I'm struggling to do that, but if I don't my marriage will die." Resist the temptation to believe that your children and your spouse can both be your first priority. It sounds good in theory, but it's impossible. Two people cannot stand in exactly the same spot.

as it should be. Further, children instinctively accept their parents' permanent loyalty to each other and not to them. In fact, they hunger for their parents to be committed to each other. In contrast, some children in stepfamilies don't accept that their parent should be permanently loyal to their stepparent and may feel insecure in response to their parent's remarriage—at least initially. Eventually they too will experience the rewards of family stability brought about by a strong marital foundation, but in the beginning they are threatened by it.

This brings us to a final temptation for you—falling prey to your child's test: "Do you love your spouse more than me?" This either/or choice feels like a no-win situation for you. Instead, think of it, as discussed earlier, as a both/and dilemma; your answer needs to reflect a deep love for *both* your children *and* your husband. You might communicate it this way to your child:

> "Sweetheart, please know that I love you with all my heart. I can see from the way you've been acting lately that you wonder if I still love you as much as I did before I remarried. You need to know that my marriage and becoming a stepmom has not changed my love for you. I know I'm not as available as I used to be, and we have less time together, but you are still my child and nothing will change that. Yet you need to know that I am choosing to love my husband and stepchildren too. It's not a competition; God has given me more than enough love for you and them. I love them differently than you, but I do love them. Know this: I will never stop loving you. You should also know that I love my husband and will always be his wife till death do us part. I am his and he is mine for life."

From time to time, children who have experienced tremendous loss and instability in life need to hear in no uncertain terms that you will never stop loving them. We all know that God loves us unconditionally, and yet we all still need to hear the words of the Lord found in Hebrews 13:5, "Never will I leave you; never will I forsake you." The permanence of love brings calm in the storm and peace to the chaos. Flood your children with it. They also need to hear that your marriage is a lifelong, never-say-die, permanent commitment that is second only to your love for the Lord. Over time, those two messages reinforced by action will keep your children from getting lost in the shuffle. It also lays the groundwork for a lifelong marriage.

MINISTERING TO YOUR CHILD'S HEART

Ministering to your children is an interesting phrase to use in reference to parenting. People use the term *ministering* when speaking of a pastor or the work of the church, but it's not usually used in regard to parenting. We are deliberate in using this word because a significant part of parenting is teaching our children moral principles for living.

Here are some concrete steps you can take to minister to your children; they are designed to keep your kids from getting lost in your stepfamily shuffle.

> ### Noncustodial Moms
>
> When you marry and your children do not live with you, there are more challenges to overcome. The good news is that today's technology provides many opportunities to stay in touch. Develop predictable routines of connecting by cell phone, text, or Internet. Remain faithful to your visitation schedule and make the most of your time together.

Remain Connected

In my book *The Smart Stepfamily*, I (Ron) tell the story of a seven-year-old girl whose mother got remarried. "What was it like for you when she got married?" I asked. She thought for a minute and replied, "You know when you're playing on the playground and a friend pushes you down and runs off and leaves you? That's what it felt like." Obviously she didn't feel as connected to her mom after the marriage as she did before.

As we've discussed throughout this book, fear is a natural

outcome of loss. It makes people—including children—hyper-sensitive to more loss. I counseled that seven-year-old's mother and new husband, so I know the mom didn't run off and leave her. But to a little girl who had already experienced a great deal of loss, it sure felt like it. Any change in the amount of time spent together or a change of emotional connection between you and your children will be felt, and perhaps exaggerated. Therefore, take intentional steps to stay connected.

> ## Adult Children
>
> Your adult children may feel jealous of your time. Maintain connections (e.g., regular phone calls, monthly lunch dates, and annual Christmas celebrations) with them and your grandchildren just as you did before marriage. When both his children and your children are together, be sure to balance your attention. Focusing too much energy on your stepkids can be a mistake.

One way is to maintain predictable activities with your children. After becoming a stepmother you will have less free time to spend with your children than you did before, but you can still be predictable in spending time with them. In addition, be emotionally predictable. Try to be the same person (e.g., personality, emotional responsiveness, and temperament) your children have come to know and now expect you to be. A radical change in mood on your part might add to their insecurity. In other words, if becoming a stepmom has turned you into a grump, it will affect your children.

Another way to stay emotionally connected with your kids is to periodically spend exclusive time with them. Compartmentalization is a useful tool for stepfamilies.[1] This involves those who are biologically related to one another spending uninterrupted time together. This provides a mini-vacation from the complications of the step relationships and brings security, togetherness, and reconnection to you and your children. We have encouraged your husband to have alone time with his kids, and it's important for you to do the same. Early in your family Crockpot you'll need to do this more often. Carve out a few hours on Sunday afternoon or find a few minutes alone with each child throughout the week. Spending this time with your children helps to reaffirm that they haven't lost you.

Maintaining *touchpoints* is another useful tool for keeping emotionally connected with your children.[2] Touchpoints are simple behaviors that communicate love and affection between people. Hugs when you greet at the end of the day, a fun handshake, and repeating a private joke shared between you and your child are all examples of touchpoints. These are very important and should be maintained even if new people in the house don't share them. Others might be invited in to these shared touchpoints but don't have to be. Stopping these behaviors communicates more loss, which can be interpreted negatively by children.

> ## When You Can't Reach Your Children
>
> When children experience hurt or rejection they may relinquish contact with a parent. No matter how hard you try, you can't reach them, and it seems fruitless. This is very frustrating and discouraging. The key is to remain consistent in trying to connect; don't harass or pester them, but clearly communicate your desire for relationship and your availability if they decide to reconnect.

Maintaining your child's social connections in familiar places where he or she feels safe is also a good way to maintain emotional connection. Any changes in your child's school, friends, church, sporting events, and/or community activities results in more loss and transition. Work diligently to refrain from these changes, especially during the first few years of the stepfamily.

A dangerous trend in today's society is single parents who begin a romance over the Internet and decide to get married. Because these parents often live in different locations, the children are quickly uprooted—sometimes sight unseen—and moved to a new city. This is a significant stressor for children, in particular if it means the loss of visitation with the biological dad.

One man wrote to Successful Stepfamilies asking if I (Ron) thought moving his fiancée's children from the East Coast to the West Coast would be okay. I could tell he was looking for permission—which I did not give. Instead I turned the tables and asked, "You've been having a long-distance relationship with your girlfriend for some time now; what if you couldn't marry her and had to permanently keep it as a long-distance relationship? How would you feel? This is what you are asking her children to do. They will be forced to try to maintain a close personal relationship with their father and other family members from the other side of the United States. Think about it."

If your marriage results in a radical shift away from the previous lifestyle your children were accustomed to, it is likely they will feel disconnected and angry. We realize that some situations require changes in the family residence. Strive to keep social changes to a bare minimum and only when absolutely necessary.

Remain Consistent

Steady, consistent parenting throughout the early stages of your stepfamily is a stabilizing factor for your children. For example, if you attended your son's football games before the wedding, make sure you continue afterward. If you and your daughter have developed a tradition of participating in the church Christmas production each year, keep that tradition alive if at all possible. Again, keep change to a minimum.

Also refrain from the temptation to pawn your kids off on a stepfather in the hopes that he can straighten them out. It's vitally important that you as the parent remain consistent in your rules, expectations, and discipline. Continue to insist, for example, that your children contribute around the home. During her single-parent years, Jennifer's children were responsible for a number of household chores. Her new husband, Matthew, had three children of his own. The two of them put their heads together and developed a new system of chores that incorporated everyone. In the end, Jennifer's kids had less work to do because there were more children to share the load, but her expectation that they contribute stayed the same.

There are some exceptions to the "stay consistent in parenting" principle. If due to exhaustion, for example, you were permissive during your single-parent years, and you allowed your children to wear you down with nagging, changes to your parenting style will be necessary. Remaining consistently inconsistent as a parent is not healthy for children. Work with your spouse to determine wise expectations or take a class on parenting to learn how to raise the standard of conduct in your home. When you as their mother begin to implement new standards, prepare for resistance and whining from your children in the beginning, and don't try to make numerous changes all at once. Ask the Lord for strength as a parent and create a new behavioral expectation in your home.

> ## Smart Dating
>
> If you are planning to marry and there are differences in your parenting styles, begin bringing your rules, consequences, and expectations in line before the wedding. This diminishes resistance from children because the change is clearly coming from you, not a stepparent.

When stepfamily dynamics necessitate a change in rules or expectations, you have another opportunity to talk openly with your kids. Liz's kids were used to watching PG-13 movies during Sunday family night. But when the visitation schedule of her husband's young children changed to include Sunday evenings, the family needed to pick more appropriate movies. Knowing her children wouldn't like the changes, Liz proactively explained the situation and communicated what they should now expect.

Changes like this can stir feelings of guilt because your decision to marry has again cost your children something (however minor it might be). Don't let this feeling paralyze you; make the change and move forward.

We have one more suggestion for maintaining consistency: If you are a co-parent, be reliable in how you cooperate with your children's father. Continue to uphold your custody and visitation arrangements, and find ways of supporting your child's relationship with the biological dad. Even if you think your husband can do a better job of parenting your children than your ex-husband does, don't diminish his role.

As a divorce recovery expert, I (Laura) have observed many women who convince themselves that the children would be better off if the biological dad were out of the picture and the stepdad became a replacement father. But unless the biological dad has a serious issue (e.g., abuse, mental illness, or addiction), this is faulty thinking and damages the children. Your kids need regular, predictable contact with their father even when they have a highly competent stepfather. Just as you can't replace your stepchildren's mother, your husband cannot replace your children's father.

> ## Making Changes
>
> During the first few years, it is generally best if biological parents manage parental changes and standards with their own children. Review chapters 7 and 8 for a discussion of the biological parent's role in discipline.

Further, if you truly love your children, you will regularly give them your verbal permission to continue loving their dad. If they feel pressured to shift their loyalties from their dad to their stepdad, you may inadvertently increase their resistance to your husband. Encouraging a relationship with their father, however, helps to facilitate a growing connection with your husband. When the relationship with your former spouse is strained, seek out skills and perspective about how to improve it. (A bank of articles addressing co-parenting is available online at *www.SuccessfulStepfamilies.com*; Laura's book *When "I Do" Becomes "I Don't"* [*www.LauraPetherbridge.com*] can also help.)

Remain an Encourager

You are your child's emotional safety blanket. Like a frightened child in the middle of the night who wraps herself in the covers to feel safe, your children will look to you for comfort when they feel insecure within the stepfamily. At that point your role is to be their soft place to fall while helping them identify feelings and emotions.

Keep in mind that relationships between stepfamily members and extended family members will develop at their own pace. Remember what we said in chapter 1? You can't force ingredients to cook at your pace. Recognize that there may be a season when new relationships are distant and cold. But steady, persistent encouragement on your part can eventually help to bridge the divide. This principle also applies when coaching your husband on how to connect with your children. The relationship between your spouse and your kids may take time to develop; you can help by gently making suggestions.

Marcus didn't share much in common with his stepbrother. Even though they were in the same grade at school, they had different interests, talents, and friends. Marcus revealed his discomfort when telling his mom that he thought Austin was "weird." His mother could see that Marcus just didn't know how to relate to Austin, so she looked for opportunities to help him relate. Over time, the two boys found some middle ground that allowed them to begin growing a relationship.

SMART QUESTIONS, SMART ANSWERS

The above principles address many common situations, but not all. Sometimes stepmoms face troubling dilemmas that need specific answers. Here are some of the most common questions Ron receives in counseling stepmoms as they relate to their own children. He has provided insightful solutions.

Smart Question: *Sometimes my stepchildren disrespect me. What do I do when my child tries to stand up for me and take on my battles?*

Smart Answer: If you discover your children trying to protect you from conflict with your husband or stepchildren, coach them out of the middle. Some children will gladly become your sergeant at arms if you let them; instead, relieve them of that duty and handle the matter yourself. After hearing her sixteen-year-old daughter berate her stepbrother for talking disrespectfully to her, one mother said to her daughter, "I appreciate that you are sticking up for me, but this is not your battle. It's mine—and I'll handle it." She concluded with a smile, "Now, go back to being a kid." The mother then addressed the situation with her stepson and talked with her husband about how they should handle his attitude. Later, she revisited the matter with her daughter and reminded her that this problem might not be resolved quickly, but that she should trust her mother and stepfather to handle it.

Smart Question: *What do I do when my husband is too harsh in punishing my children?*

Smart Answer: First, understand that our answer assumes your husband is not being abusive. No home should include angry, violent discipline from either parent. If there is violence, call the police and put a stop to it. Then get counsel from a professional.

Your question indicates that you don't agree with the type of discipline your husband is implementing. He may be loud when he disciplines or overly punitive with consequences (e.g., "You're grounded for six months!"). First, gently try to help him understand that his poor choice is putting a wedge in his relationship with his stepchildren. Unless you agree on how to discipline, his style will be experienced as mean or uncaring by your children. Again, wisdom would suggest he stop while you take over being the primary parent.

Second, you must negotiate a set of parental responses on which you can agree in order to build unity in your marriage and harmony in the home. If repeated discussions do not result in agreement, take the matter outside your marriage. Attend a class together or seek counsel from a parent educator or therapist so you can develop a shared system of parenting.

Smart Question: *What if my husband has expectations for my children that he doesn't have for his own?*

Smart Answer: As referenced above, either you haven't negotiated common expectations for all the children, or your husband won't follow through with your mutual decisions. If you haven't done the former, attend to it immediately. You will continue to be divided until you do. If, however, you have negotiated expectations but your husband won't follow through, bring the inconsistency to his attention in a soft manner. It's likely that he is afraid or paralyzed by guilt; harshly accusing him of favoring his children or not accepting yours is premature. Ask and listen.

Say something such as, "Honey, I'm confused about some things and hope you can help me understand. We have discussed and decided what we expect from the children, but you seem to get stuck when trying to follow through with your children. I know I have been defensive about this before, but I'm trying hard not to be now. Do you know what holds you back?" Hopefully he has an awareness of his barriers and will share them with you. Handle his feelings with care, or he won't share them again.

Smart Question: *What do I do when my husband disrespects me in front of my children?*

Smart Answer: Gently and respectfully say, "Please don't talk to me that way. Now, let's continue our conversation in private." Self-respect is maintained when partners assertively set boundaries with each other. When your children hear you say, "Please don't talk to me that way," they will learn that standing up for yourself is not a sin. At the same time, a respectful tone toward your husband teaches that we don't have to get out of control when offended. This too is a good lesson for children to learn.

Smart Question: *How do I explain to my children why my husband changes into a different person when his children come for the weekend?*

Smart Answer: Understandably, noncustodial parents often find an extra measure of tolerance, flexibility, and cheerfulness when their children come to visit. They want to make the most of the time available and leave the children feeling good about their visit. It is likely that your children have experienced this themselves either from you or their father; use that experience to explain what is happening with their stepfather.

You might say, "I'm sure it's confusing that your stepfather acts differently or lets his children get away with stuff he would never let you get away with. We need to understand that he is just trying to enjoy time with his children and that he misses them. He feels bad that he doesn't get to see them more often. I'm like that when you come back from being at your dad's all summer; I'm so happy you're back that I don't worry about you making your bed every day, right? It may be hard to understand, but that's what he is doing. I know it feels unfair, but try not to take it personally. What if we talked to him together about how this makes you feel?"

Smart Question: *What do I do when my children feel left out or unimportant to my husband?*

Smart Answer: Some children desire a deeper relationship with their stepfather than he does with them. This creates a difficult dilemma for the child. It's not uncommon for your child to experience some disappointment when the stepdad spends one-on-one time with his children. However, a child who is repeatedly pushed aside will experience great discouragement.

Once you become aware of your child's feelings, share them with your husband. Approaching him with blame or accusations of being unloving will inflame his defenses. Seek, rather, to communicate what is happening, and help him discover why he is remaining distant. Then explore how he might find ways to connect with the child. If after doing so your husband will not make changes, like a single parent you will have to continue being the primary nurturer for your child, coaching them through their disappointment (see the section on emotional coaching in chapter 4), and hugging their hurt.

If he remains disengaged with your children, find other male mentors who can fill some of the gaps. And finally, guard your heart from resenting your husband to a level that breaks down your commitment to him. Losing respect for him would be understandable, but don't allow your disappointment to erode your marriage completely.

SURVIVING THE STEPFAMILY FOREST

Therapists and stepfamily educators John and Emily Visher used to joke that stepfamilies don't have a family tree, they have a family forest! As seedlings in your forest, your children can easily get lost among the towering trees and foliage. A little extra water and warm sunshine from you can do wonders.

PRAYER

Dear Lord,

You know I love my children. I would do anything for them. When I look into those sweet eyes and see their precious smiles, I can hardly contain my emotions. I never knew I could love like this. All of this is why I desire to do what is best for my children. If I wasn't ready to accept or I didn't understand the changes they would face due to my remarriage, please forgive me.

Teach me, Lord, how to honor my spouse without alienating or harming my kids. Show me the best way to love and parent them as a godly mother. My desire to protect them is such a powerful emotion that I'm not always certain I'm making the best choices.

Teach me how to encourage them in all their relationships, including the ones with their biological dad, my spouse, their siblings, and their stepsiblings.

I trust you in every circumstance. Thank you for loving my children even more than I do and for promising to guide me in this task. Amen.

PRAYER REFERENCES

Isaiah 43:5; 49:15; 54:13   *Proverbs 31:28*

Luke 18:16   *Psalm 103:13, 17*

Ephesians 6:1–4

Smart Stepmom Discussion Questions

1. What are your feelings about how your marriage has affected your children?

2. Fear typically paralyzes us; therefore, it's vitally important to recognize what triggers your "fear factor." What are your fears concerning your children? How do these fears impact you as a parent?

3. Which of the following are temptations for you?

   - Underestimating your child's adjustments and losses
   - Being more a mother than a wife

4. What is the most difficult part about making your marriage a priority? What issues regarding this are causing guilt feelings? What actions does that lead you to take?

5. How have you remained connected with your children? What are some ways you can remain more closely attached?

6. What is your children's relationship with their biological father? Are you helping to strengthen that relationship? What steps can you take to do so?

7. What is your children's relationship with your husband? In what realistic ways would you like to see it improve?

8. How have you stayed emotionally and parentally consistent with your children through the transition to marriage?

9. How are you coping with any negative effects your children may be experiencing due to this marriage? Are you seeking resources, workshops, or materials that might help you to ease their pain? Is your husband willing to participate?

10. In what ways have you been able to encourage your children regarding the stepfamily? What improvements might you make? What areas that are out of your control must you accept as part of the stepfamily dynamic?

Chapter 11

Kodak Moments: Vacations, Holidays, Mother's Day, and Special Occasions

Whether we are seven or seventy, women usually enjoy getting dressed up. I (Laura) think it has something to do with the fact that a special occasion provides an excuse for buying a new pair of shoes. However, as fun as they are, special occasions can produce anxiety. The number of people involved in a stepfamily and the increase of complications can intensify the stress factor.

Stepmom Sherrie explains the situation to her sister. "Amy, if you think the holidays are hectic at your house, try coordinating schedules, decorating, shopping, school programs, dinner, and gift giving with the parents of three households. Add to the mix that most of the adults involved don't even like each other, and you have a taste of what Christmas is like in a stepfamily. Everything is more complicated because there are so many people who influence the plans, including the biological mom, her parents and siblings, and her husband's family. Many of these people don't share our priorities, so coordinating is like trying to hit a moving target."

The multiple-home, multiple-parent, multiple-grandparent, and in-law complexities of a stepfamily often rise to the surface during special occasions. The collision of various traditions, preferences, and cultural norms can produce an interesting dynamic. In addition, it seems that holidays and special occasions bring out the best and the worst in people. The stepmom often feels the brunt of the entire experience because the planning of family holidays and celebrations often falls on her.[1] A stepmom may feel overwhelmed and shocked by the flurry of activity and the sudden responsibility to coordinate everything. Our goal for this chapter is to help you understand the dynamics that are at play, plus offer practical survival tips.

HOLIDAY DYNAMICS

Connections That Endure

Holidays and special occasions are stressful because they serve an important function for families. They facilitate family identity and belonging. And there's the rub for a stepmom: When she feels outside of the family circle, these special events can throw gasoline on an existing flame; the event can magnify her loneliness and discomfort.

Traditions also play a huge role in the holiday dynamic. When family rituals and customs are sustained, they reinforce family identity and define what is normal or customary behavior for the special day. I (Laura) grew up in a large Italian family (on my dad's side). Cooking was Nana's reason for living, and Christmas Eve was her masterpiece. She made enough meatballs, calamari, and biscotti to feed an army. On that night her house was packed with friends and relatives, and you could hear the laughter and smell the garlic from a block away. Those are wonderful childhood memories for me, which I'd love to pass on to my stepsons. But they already have their own traditions, based on family background. What feels cozy and familiar to me isn't normal for them. This lack of shared tradition makes each side feel different, disconnected, and separate, thereby generating discomfort and stress for everyone.

Bridging the gap is the goal for the stepfamily. This usually requires slowly implementing new traditions while holding on to old ones. Just as taking the bread and wine during Communion symbolizes that we belong to the body of Christ, new family traditions can symbolize and create a connection.

For example, the first summer you take the family water-skiing it is an exciting new adventure. The fourth time you go it becomes "something we do every year." Feel the difference? Vacations, holidays, and special family celebrations hold great opportunity for you and your husband to cook your stepfamily.

What Lies Beneath

The life of the Smart Stepmom is a daily journey. You may have conquered feelings of anger, frustration, and loneliness, but the differences in how you'd like to celebrate special occasions may bring sadness back to the surface. If your vacation idea or tradition is quickly squashed by your stepkids because they view it as strange, their response may resurrect a wound and the feeling of being an outsider. Take a moment to gather your thoughts, and remember that they are not rejecting you personally, it's merely one more adjustment or change that the kids are shunning. A change in tradition or custom is one more loss for kids who have lost a parent or experienced divorce.

Toxic Circumstances

When several family members who are unsettled about the stepfamily are gathered together for a special occasion, the cumulative anxiety may create an explosion. The underlying raw emotions that each person carries may be inflamed by others in the room. Therefore, take caution before throwing numerous family members into close surroundings if you suspect they are incapable of handling the tension. It's best to celebrate separately until these issues can be resolved. Trying to resolve family conflict during special occasions is usually unproductive. Ask your husband for suggestions on how to diffuse the problem in the future. You may need a counselor or a third party who can objectively help you understand how to make plans for future family events.

Adult Stepchildren

When parents and adult children live a great distance from one another, special events may be the only practical "cooking time" with stepchildren. At the same time, the natural anxiety of gathering everyone in one place may irritate sensitivities. Intentionally use these occasions to build relationships with family members, but keep the expectations low.

Another situation that can cause a problem is when you and the former wife agree on a schedule but your husband refuses to compromise. Gail shares, "It's easier if I try to work things out with my stepson's mom than if my husband does it. We get our calendars coordinated and plot it all out and get it in writing. If we need to make changes later, we're flexible as much as possible. But this rarely works because my husband is not willing to give up control and refrain from demanding his way. Then the situation turns back to yelling and screaming, and everyone suffers."

Power Plays

One of the most difficult situations that can arise during special events is the power struggle between biological parents. Even former spouses who typically get along fairly well may burst into anger and start fighting. Here are a few of the most common emotions and power plays a stepmom may experience during special events:

- Aggravation when waiting for the biological mom to decide the holiday schedule for both homes

- Annoyance when a biological mom changes all of the plans at the last minute

- Frustration over the biological mom who refuses to abide by the visitation schedule legally established in a divorce agreement

- Stress over grandparents who refuse to recognize the complexities of a stepfamily

- Sadness when the ever-present memory of a deceased mother is so highly honored that new traditions, meals, or decorations cannot be presented

- Anger when extended family members voice their disapproval of the stepfamily to the children during family get-togethers

These dynamics can make a stepmom feel helpless and weary. Here are a few smart steps to help curb the conflict and tension.

First, pay attention to the tiptoe dance that might be causing stress, and do what you can to change it. One woman described their dance this way: "Because he is on edge and doesn't want to deal with his ex-wife, he procrastinates in finding out details about the schedule. This causes tension between us when I ask what the plans are because if he has not spoken to her yet, he gets defensive and mad at me. We are always tiptoeing around each other, wondering if the next event will blow up like others have." Talk with your husband and openly discuss this type of dance in a calm manner. For example, review how you have previously handled the stress without fighting. Then develop an action plan and try to stick with it. It might sound like this: "Honey, I know that talking to your ex-wife about holiday schedules is very stressful for you. I'm also aware that when I ask you what the plans are, it sounds as if I'm judging you for not talking to her. I certainly don't mean to judge you or make you feel pressured. How can I best ask you about this in the future and support you?"

Second, choose between-home battles carefully. Whenever possible, attempt to live in peace with the other home. This will require making sacrifices so the children don't have to deal with warring parents. This may seem unfair if your family is making all of the concessions, but this is the reality of a stepfamily. On occasion, however, there are battles that need to be engaged. The difficulty is learning when to deal with the issue and when to let it go. If the biological mom, for example, normally is flexible about the holiday schedule, but for some reason this year she is unwilling to bend, then let it go. But if she has a pattern of repeatedly ignoring the divorce arrangement and refusing to allow visitation, or if she controls the children's time, that's probably a boundary worth battling. She is being unreasonable and hurting the kids. Accommodating her antics gives her more power and increases resentment within your home.

Will fighting these battles result in repercussions? Most likely. However, your husband (note: not you) needs to calmly notify the biological mom that she is repeatedly ignoring the legal visitation agreement, and if she continues, he will take legal action against her. Understand that the process may become difficult and the kids may be angry. However, it is necessary to break the cycle of behavior. In addition, the children need to know that their dad loves them enough to fight for his time with them. No matter how bad the battle, try to keep the children out of the conflict. If the biological mom chooses to inflict turmoil on her children, you cannot control her choices, but do everything you can to avoid putting them in the middle of the conflict. It must be between your spouse and his former wife.

In the same regard, if you ask the parents of your husband's deceased wife to buy gifts equally for both their grandchildren and stepgrandchildren, or not buy any gifts at all, this will likely ruffle their feathers and reverberate throughout the family system. It's still the right thing to do. A little discomfort now can prevent a lot of resentment and hard feelings later. While gift considerations should be equitable, time considerations may be different. There is nothing wrong with a grandparent who desires special time with a biological grandchild, especially if this is balanced with time spent with the entire stepfamily.

When power plays occur within your home, strive to model a spirit of compromise. If children are old enough to have an opinion, call a family meeting. For example, discuss how you will open presents on Christmas morning. It's unwise to allow an "our way is right" attitude from children. Instead encourage them to listen to one another and try to incorporate something old and something new into the family tradition. Finally, when possible give permission for different expressions and styles even within your own home; don't insist that everyone do everything the same.

Comparisons

In a stepfamily it's easy to get caught up in a vicious cycle of comparison. "My kids only get to decorate one Christmas tree, his get two. Why should mine have to wait for his to come back from their mom's before they can decorate the tree?" Making this decision simply because "his kids get two trees and that's not fair" is unwise. In the end, this may be the best decision for your family, but it should be evaluated and decided for a number of reasons, not due to household comparisons.

Money Considerations

Because stepfamilies tend to be large, buying gifts for special occasions and Christmas can overload the stepfamily budget. Stepfamily educators Jeff and Judi Parziale point out, "Stresses mount as families attempt to stretch an already tight budget or decide for whom (and for whom not) to buy gifts. Parents argue over differing traditions and spending limits. Children gripe about having to buy presents for stepsiblings (or stepparents) they barely know, and may not even like."[2]

Creative solutions to these stressors include not insisting that children buy a gift for everyone, setting an overall family spending limit, drawing names for gifts, and focusing on fairness in purchases.

Another area that can cause stress is comparing vacations between the households. One stepmom wrote, "Vacations! Ha! What's that? Since their mom has taken us back to court twice we can't afford to take a nice vacation, but she sure can. This past summer we didn't get to do anything. My husband took his kids fishing for a few days, but that was the extent of our vacation. On the other hand, the biological mom and stepdad took them to a lake house and spent the entire week on their boat having a great time. It drives me crazy. We cannot afford to do anything because of *her*, but she can afford anything and everything. I just don't understand our court system."

> ### When Mom Is Deceased
>
> When family traditions are modified or omitted, one fear children may experience is that Mom is being forgotten. We recommend that you keep at least one significant tradition alive that honors the children's mother. This shows your respect for her, demonstrates that you are not taking her place, and honors their grief. As they mature, stepchildren usually develop a great appreciation for your efforts to keep their mom's memory alive.

This stepmom's bitterness is apparent. Even if her reasoning is justified, her attitude won't bring anything but unrest. To be absolutely clear, a father is required by law, but even more important by God's Word, to provide emotionally and financially for his children (see 1 Timothy 5:8). His decision to remarry does not minimize or nullify his responsibility to his children. If the law or a judge's decision has been unfair to him, the solution is to obtain a new lawyer and go back to court. But making financial comparisons as this woman did won't change anything, and it makes everyone in the situation stressed. When you choose to marry a man with children, you choose to deal with a former wife and circumstances that are out of your control.

Increased Fear and Mixed Emotions

While holidays and special family occasions stir warm feelings for most people, others experience sadness and pain. "My former husband was an abusive man," shared Debbie, "and it all came to a head around Christmas; that's when my teenage children and I left him and started over. Each year after my divorce, Christmastime became a mixed bag of emotions—both bitter and sweet. I even find myself wondering if my current husband will hurt us." These fears and others like them may be normal for a season. You may need to talk with a mentor or trusted friend. Ask God to reveal the areas where fear may be holding you hostage and keeping you from enjoying special occasions.

Stepsiblings

Stepsiblings may have a variety of responses during special occasions. For example, Kathy shared how her teenage stepchildren made fun of her younger children's traditions. "For the first couple years my husband and I had to remind his kids that these were their Christmas traditions and were worthy of respect. My husband really had to stay on them so they wouldn't belittle my children." Because traditions define who we are and what is normal, this type of circumstance is somewhat predictable. Thankfully, Kathy's husband was willing to speak up for his stepchildren and not allow his children to talk down to them.

Children who are given many material possessions may try to make stepsiblings jealous. Toni learned to prepare her daughter for how her stepsiblings would flaunt the gifts they received from a wealthy aunt. She worked hard to teach her daughter an appreciation for the gifts she received and discussed how not to resent her step-siblings even though their materialistic attitudes were misguided.

Stress during family occasions may arise when children are troubled over the fact that they can't be with certain family members. Being with one side of the family usually means not being with someone else. Jolene was her husband's third wife, and he had two children with each of the three women. The children from his previous marriages didn't get much time with their father, which produced jealousy toward Jolene's children, who lived with him full time. When holidays rolled around, her stepchildren called attention to themselves in order to spend extra time with their father. Jolene sympathized with their situation, but the way they would compare or criticize others in order to stand out was of great concern to her.

Step Money

Money is a tool. Since having a lot of money never quenches our thirst for more, placing it in its rightful place on life's priority list is very wise. Few people look back on their lives and wish they'd had more money. Instead we prize our relationships and the love we shared. Live today to store up treasures in heaven.

While it is appropriate to set boundaries with children in order to promote fairness and a positive spirit, understand that the underlying problem in this setting is a distant relationship with Dad. Keep in mind that children are in part products of their environment and parenting; if they act obnoxious, it is likely they have been allowed to do so, or they are hurting emotionally. You may not have a parenting voice with every child, but you can protect and coach your children toward better behavior.

Broken Connections

Holidays and special family events bring to light broken relationships. Alienated parents and children, for example, will feel their loss more intensely during these occasions. If your husband has a strained relationship with his child, when that child's birthday approaches he will likely experience loss and pain—and so will the child. But these occasions can also offer hope. Part of the magic of special family occasions is the extra motivation people acquire to set aside differences, offer forgiveness, and find reconciliation. Set an example of this spirit for your husband and stepchildren. Many distant relationships are restored when one person is nudged toward the other.

Mother's Day

If there is one day of the year that can trigger either elation or sadness for a stepmom, it's usually Mother's Day. The day can be uncomfortable for everyone. My (Laura) husband wants to honor me on this day for loving his kids, but he isn't always sure how. My stepsons call and wish me a happy Mother's Day, but we both know I'm not their mom, so it feels awkward. I do not expect my stepsons to honor me on Mother's Day—because I'm NOT their mom. However, I do desire for my husband to do something nice, such as take me out for brunch, as a gesture of gratitude for all the years of working toward building a bridge with his kids.

One stepmom shared a similar feeling. "For years I've tried to explain to my spouse that Mother's Day was a day for *him* to show me how much he appreciated my being a good stepmother to his daughter. It took a few years, but he finally got it. The worst year was when he called his former wife and asked her to have their daughter call me the Monday afterward to say happy Mother's Day. I was furious. I told him that when she was an adult she was more than welcome to call me or send a card, but as long as she was a child, I wanted *him* to make it a special day for me while she shared the day with her mom. Forcing her to call me just seemed weird."

Another stepmom shared this experience: "My husband has tried some goofy stuff for Mother's Day. One year he bought a bouquet of flowers and had the kids split them, half for his former wife and half for me. The hurtful part is that I remember when we were dating he would take the kids shopping for extravagant gifts for his ex, but it's the Dollar Store for me—not pretty."

One of the reasons Mother's Day produces so much emotion is because many stepmoms feel that they have all of the pain, frustrations, negative emotions, financial strain, and difficulty of being a parent, but none of the joys. As one stepmom put it, "I get all the grief of parenting, but I don't get to enjoy the pleasures associated with being a mom."

On the other hand, some stepmoms experience a wonderful day. "My first Mother's Day, his girls took me out for breakfast. While we were eating they gave me a beautiful card, with wording that was extremely touching. It brought tears to my eyes, and I started to cry. The youngest, age fourteen, also cried. She really made me feel special by recognizing my deep feelings on Mother's Day."

It's not uncommon for one specific hour on Mother's Day to be the worst time of the day for stepmoms. I (Laura) used to dread going to church that day. This situation can be extremely painful and uncomfortable as the church honors moms. Elaine shares this: "The way our pastor says 'mothers,' you know he only means those by birth. He has the women come forward, and then he prays a blessing upon them. As a stepmom this has always been an awkward moment for me. Many people in the church have made sure I go up front, and they assure me that I am a mom. This year was still a bit awkward, but I told myself that I know in my heart I am a mom, so with that, I was going to be proud." She asked, "What about foster parents, adoptive parents, or an aunt caring for her nieces and nephews? Don't they matter?" Our answer: absolutely.

> ## A Mother's Day Script for Pastors
>
> "This morning is Mother's Day, a time to honor God's gift we call 'Mom.' If you are a mother, a stepmother, an adoptive mother, a foster mother, or a woman who cares for children in any capacity, would you please stand so we can honor you this morning."

206 The **Smart** Stepmom

For years Ron has encouraged church leaders to acknowledge stepmothers on Mother's Day. "Just use the word *stepmom*," he tells them, "and you validate her as an important caregiver in her home and remind her stepchildren that they too should give her thanks for what she does." Having this sensitivity may seem obvious to you and us, but it is far from the minds of most pastors because they don't know how confusing Mother's Day is for both children and parents. They assume all women who mother children are given equal consideration as part of the Mother's Day celebration—but, of course, they are not. Consider educating your preacher or church leaders about the complications of Mother's Day for stepmothers; perhaps you could take them to lunch a month or so before Mother's Day and share your heart. We find that once enlightened, many pastors are more than willing to acknowledge stepmothers during Mother's Day and other special occasions.

Vacations

"Early in our marriage I hoped to take a vacation and visit my family," stepmom Susan shared. "The kids are big war buffs so I thought the boys would enjoy the nearby museums and monuments, plus my dad has a large collection of WWII items. But at the last minute the kids decided they didn't want to go. I was very hurt and felt humiliated and disappointed."

Stepfamily complications often arise during vacations because a collision of two cultures occurs. When your ideas of what constitutes a great vacation collide with your spouse and his children's, it is easy to feel rejected or isolated. Differing concepts of family fun can create stress and division.

For example, walking around the rim of the Grand Canyon for five hours may be fun for your spouse and his kids, but a nightmare for you. When this occurs, it is important to realize that this is merely a matter of preference and not necessarily a personal rejection of you or a reflection of your relationship with his kids.

My (Laura) idea of a fun time is relaxing in a historic or scenic place, being on a cruise and doing some snorkeling in the Caribbean, or shopping in quaint stores. But my stepkids don't like any of those things. Therefore, my husband and I have discovered that it's wise for us to take a few days for ourselves doing the things we enjoy together, and then we also have family time with his kids and grandkids. This year we went to Sea World in Orlando the day after Christmas (the busiest time of the year). I wasn't overjoyed to spend the day in a crowded theme park, but it was what they wanted to do. I prayed before we left and asked God to help me focus on how much fun my husband has with his grandkids and how fortunate we are to have worked through many of the difficulties of a stepfamily. This shift in focus allowed me to enjoy the day, Shamu, and time with family.

One key to success is having a private conversation with your spouse before a vacation or event and reviewing when potential pitfalls may occur. Then communicate these issues with the children to create a shared expectation for your time together. One Smart Stepmom shared the following with her adult stepchildren as they planned several vacation days together, including a day-long event that she knew would be exhausting for her and her husband. "We are so excited to spend time with you. Please understand that we probably won't have the energy or the stamina to make it through the entire day. We plan to enjoy the day with you, and then when we get tired we will take a break. Please know this is not a protest of the activity; it's about our endurance. We don't want to ruin the day for you, so feel free to make your plans, and we will join you as we're able."

This type of honest conversation may flow easily in a biological family. But in a stepfamily where the relationships aren't fully formed, the question of "How honest can I be?" often lurks beneath the surface. We tend to consent to the wants of others rather than honestly share our feelings. This can create tension and resentment, in particular if the trip involves a great expense. Before the vacation or activity it's wise to effectively communicate in a way that gives permission for differences or preference and allows both parties to set boundaries on participation.

Weddings

If you are planning on receiving recognition or playing a significant role in your stepchild's wedding, then prepare yourself for potential disappointment. Daughters in particular desire to have a perfect wedding day. For many this means having their biological mother and father appear normal at the wedding. It provides them with a sense of family, and for a few hours it erases the shame, dysfunction, and chaos associated with broken families.

My (Laura) suggestion to stepmoms is to offer help with a bridal shower, or any other task the bride or groom needs done, but even if you have spent years raising this child, do not expect to be placed in a strategic role on the wedding day. If the child chooses to honor you, that is wonderful; enjoy the glory. But guard your heart; if you expect admiration for all your hard work, you may end up wounded. Although it's difficult to do, lower your expectations. Understand that it's totally normal for a stepchild who typically showers you with love and respect to become distant and aloof while planning a wedding.

Full Circle

We'd like to offer a word of encouragement about the nature of holidays, vacations, and special family occasions. Despite the many complications stepfamily life brings to these occasions, they may also provide stepmoms with an opportunity to come full circle in the eyes of the children. Have you ever noticed that the older we become, the wiser our parents seem to have been all along? That same life perspective can elevate the status of stepmoms. Children who have taken you for granted for years or resented your presence may realize during an annual family vacation just how central you have become to their life. Once children become parents, they may discover how fortunate they were to have you for a stepmom. One glowing stepmom received this note from her youngest stepson a few years after he started his own family. "Mom, I'm sitting here looking at our Christmas tree and it is reminding me of how special you always made Christmas. Thanks for taking the trouble to get a real tree every year. I know I took those things for granted, but I now realize how much you did for us. See you in a couple weeks."

This kind of appreciation may not come quickly, but trust that as you keep your eyes on Christ and follow his example, it will make an impact on your stepchildren who observe your godly choices.

PRACTICAL STRATEGIES

The first half of this chapter offered perspective for coping with the emotional and relational issues of special family occasions. Now we move on to the practical. Here are some smart strategies to help smooth the pavement.

Father Leadership

This paragraph is for your husband. Dads, now that you are remarried, you need to take a proactive initiative when it comes to managing between-home schedules with your former wife, your household, and your extended family. Many men are shocked to discover that the passive, "go along with what everyone else wants" strategy they employed during

Smart Dating

Dad, even before the wedding you can begin implementing these strategies should you decide to spend holidays together. Slowly work the future stepparent into established rituals and begin looking for new traditions that connect everyone. These you will want to keep after the wedding!

their single-parent years is counter-productive once they remarry. Previously this method kept everyone happy; now it angers almost everyone, especially your wife. Dad, if this has been you, it's time to get off the bench and play quarterback. Take the initiative to make difficult phone calls and set boundaries (that is, say no) when necessary. Be certain to communicate expectations to your own extended family members, and set priorities with your travel schedule that honor your wife first, then your children, then your extended family. Attempting to find a solution when numerous people are pulling on you and desire their own way can be extremely stressful. Therefore, it's crucial that you communicate calmly and effectively with your wife; share your needs and listen to hers. Then you will be equipped to make tough decisions. This is the way to win the respect of your wife and head off any number of family disputes. Engage.

Plan, Plan, Plan

As a couple, be proactive in discussing upcoming holiday events. Stress results when families fail to plan and then try to play catch-up with all that needs to be done. For example, a clearly articulated visitation schedule is helpful to everyone impacted. Stepmother Linda shared, "Things always work best when we have a plan that has been spelled out in detail, and all parties (ex-spouses, grandparents, and children) are aware of it. Then there's no guesswork, misunderstandings, miscommunications, or hurt feelings."

Carpe Diem

Solomon, the wisest man who ever lived, encourages us in the book of Ecclesiastes to live every moment to its fullest and to enjoy the present rather than rehashing the past or getting lost in the future. For some this means celebrating special days when you can, even if it's not the actual day. "We celebrate Christmas the week before," said

Diane. "It's the only way we can celebrate it on our terms. It isn't quite the same as opening presents on Christmas Day, but we make it fun for everyone and really throw ourselves into it." Smart Stepmoms realize that enthusiasm and a positive spirit make alternatives like this possible. When you don't have a choice, make the most of your options.

For other stepmoms, carpe diem means not waiting for everyone before celebrating with those present. Melissa found a good option for her family through trial and error. "Even when we planned ahead, his ex-wife would change the visitation schedule at the last minute. Then we would hold off on decorating the tree and doing fun family activities till his children were there. My husband and I realized that we were imprisoned by his ex-wife's irresponsibility, waiting to live life until she made it okay for us to do so. It was hurting us and our daughter. We always try to include all the kids, but now we also move forward whether everyone is there or not—and we enjoy our time without feeling guilty."

Prepare You

Spending time with the One who gives strength in times of stress, and seeking his wisdom, is an essential act of preparation for stepmoms. Dedicate extra time to prayer before certain events and ask others to pray for you.

While outward appearances don't make the woman, they can boost your self-esteem as you face uncertain circumstances. Occasionally dote on yourself a bit before stressful events. Make a hair appointment, have a manicure or facial—whatever will boost your self-confidence a notch.[3]

Be Flexible, Make Sacrifices, and Have a Backup Plan

Being flexible means having the willingness to modify an old tradition to bring an outside stepfamily member in. It also means being flexible in working through stepfamily dilemmas. On occasion you will have to make sacrifices; for example, when an ex-wife-in-law insists that it is her job to bring the birthday cake. Don't keep score of sacrifices and always have a backup plan in case you need one.

Be Inclusive

You may not have chosen all the members of your multiple-household family, but choosing to welcome, embrace, and love them is a gift to everyone—especially yourself. Some stepmoms try to exclude certain family members from special occasions. Avoid this temptation, and if at all possible include members from the other biological family. This builds a bridge and can provide the freedom children enjoy when all of their family members are present at one event. We realize this may not be possible in every situation, especially if there is still bitterness after a divorce. However, many of the most accepted and content stepmoms have an open, hospitable spirit that extends grace and welcomes others. Remain pleasant and inviting with those who are connected to your stepchildren (even if you don't care for them), and show your children that love is not competitive.

Give Permission

Give the children your permission to enjoy the other household and all their family members. When a stepmother and father say, "I'm thrilled that you will be spending time with your mom and stepdad over Christmas. Have lots of fun!" you are releasing them from guilt and worry over how you will fare during their absence.

Honor Traditions

Maintaining old traditions can be more difficult given the shifting presence of family members. Keep the ones you can and look for ways to establish new traditions.

Live and Learn

One couple found themselves disappointed year after year because the children had to be rushed off to the other house in the middle of Christmas Day. They were never able to fully enjoy the day because everyone was watching the clock. Eventually they proposed a change to the biological mom. As it turned out, she was also discouraged each Christmas and was open to changing the visitation agreement. They settled on an alternating arrangement that gave each home an undisturbed Christmas holiday while the other home had an undisturbed Thanksgiving holiday. The loss of togetherness experienced during one holiday was moderated by the joy they received during the other. Not all stepfamily decisions have clear solutions; sometimes you must simply live and learn. This requires letting go of control and trusting God to whittle away what doesn't work so you can learn what does. Open communication with your husband throughout the trial-and-error period is important. Strive not to blame each other for the errors. Instead process them and try again.

Don't Sweat the Small Stuff

You can't do it all. Let priorities dictate what you are able to do and what you can't; then let go of the small stuff. Don't worry about the things that need to occur but you as the stepmom can't control. Give those tasks back to your husband. This is not failing in your role, nor is it passive-aggressive. It simply shifts responsibility back to your husband—who has the power to manage the details of his children's lives—and frees you to focus on the issues within your influence.

Over time family holidays and special occasions have the power to define, maintain, and renew your family's identity and connection to one another. The traditions and rituals found in these special family events give meaning and direction to your life together. Be intentional as each occasion presents an opportunity to deepen your family connections and inspire hope for the future.

PRAYER

Lord, you left heaven and came to earth to provide salvation and hope for a broken and dying world. You love me so much that you were willing to leave the glory of heaven to save my soul by dying on the cross for my sins. Although I once walked in darkness and death, your birth and amazing grace have provided me with light and life. My gratitude is overflowing. You alone are my Wonderful Counselor, Mighty God, Everlasting Father, and the Prince of Peace.

Lord, I desire to create enjoyable memories with my husband and stepchildren. Teach us how to set aside the things that cause dissension and focus on the positive. Create in me an ability to understand that not everything my stepchildren do or say is a reflection of their opinions about me.

Help us, Lord, to focus on you during these special occasions. And when things aren't going as I planned or other people interfere and cause strife, give me the mind of Christ so I may respond as you would. Help me to focus on your unfailing love. May it be my comfort according to your promise. I want more of you and less of my self-interest.

Thank you for hearing my prayer. I'm grateful that your love for me can't be shaken or removed. I worship you with all of my heart. Amen.

PRAYER REFERENCES

John 3:16–17   *Psalm 48:9*
Luke 2:10–11   *Psalm 119:76*
Romans 5:8   *Isaiah 54:10*
Isaiah 9:2, 6

Smart Stepmom Discussion Questions

1. What complications associated with stepfamily special occasions have taken you by surprise over the years?

2. How does knowing that traditions define family identity help you understand the strong emotional responses of yourself and others?

3. What new traditions has your family created already? What are some that you are working on?

4. Have you felt sadness or witnessed others in the family feeling depressed during special occasions? How might you respond?

5. Which power plays by the biological mom, grandparents, extended family, or others do you experience during special events? Which have you and/or your husband been guilty of?

6. What money considerations are especially troublesome for your stepfamily?

7. What fears do family special events elicit in you? What are specific ways you can tame or manage those emotions?

8. What stepsibling issues are you facing? What possible answers did you get from this chapter?

9. How might you implement some of the practical strategies listed? Do they give you hope or explain what is normal?

10. As a group, discuss specific ways you can cope with days such as Mother's Day. Also talk about how to lower your expectations and better manage vacations, holidays, and special events in ways that relieve stress.

Chapter 12

Adult Stepchildren

*The middle daughter goes to church with us almost every Sun-
day, and she and I are growing into good friends. The other two
are very angry and stuck. It is miserable to be around them.*
                              Stepmother of stepchildren
                              ages 26, 24, 20

———

*I am now the outsider in what used to be my own family. . . . I
feel incredibly alone.*
                              Adult stepdaughter age 31

———

*Dad, you are losing yourself in this new relationship. I want the
dad I know, not the man you think she wants you to be.*
                              Adult stepdaughter age 37

Did you know that some studies indicate that later-in-life remarriages
can be more satisfying than earlier marriages? At least two studies
suggest that a couple can develop healthy communication patterns
that were absent in their first marriages, thereby contributing to
greater marital satisfaction.[1] So here's the good news: An empty nest

paired with positive couple interaction can result in a wonderful marital experience in later life.

This chapter targets stepfamilies that initially formed after the children were adults (over the age of eighteen). It is certainly true that stepfamilies formed with minor-age children will have unique challenges after the children become adults. However, we are limiting our discussion here to the unique transitional issues associated with adult stepfamilies.

Warning and word of caution: If you saw this chapter title in the table of contents and started reading here, we strongly advise that you begin with chapter 1. Most of the key principles addressed throughout this book apply to adult stepfamilies too. The specific complaints from adult stepchildren are somewhat different from those of younger children (e.g., inheritance issues); however, the essential feelings, fears, and concerns are very similar.

For example, the principle of patience is equally important for adult stepfamilies. It's possible you may need even more patience than younger stepfamilies since "cooking time" is dependent upon how much time you spend with the stepchildren. Some adult stepfamilies are spread out across great distances, which makes it even more difficult to build relationships. In addition, the matters of loss and loyalty (chapters 4 and 5) are just as salient for adult stepchildren as they are for younger children. Other principles, such as those addressing parenting, may not apply to your situation. But in general we encourage you to consider the entire book valuable information for your family.

If your husband was widowed, you may be tempted to dismiss principles that seem to apply to divorced families. Again, most principles have application to you and your adult stepfamily. Therefore, for those of you who skipped several chapters in this book and zeroed in on this one, it's likely that you'll finish it feeling that pieces or solutions are missing. That's because many of the dynamics of adult stepfamilies are addressed in other chapters.

Even though later-life marriages can be satisfying, stepfamily complexities still exist even when there are no small children or teens. Many empty-nest couples mistakenly assume that a second marriage will be smooth sailing.

One stepmother, Carol, submitted her story, hoping to find some answers.

Two years ago I married a widower. I am forty-seven, he is forty-nine. . . . Because we felt God put us together and were sure of the relationship . . . we married eight months after our first date.

I have no children but love kids. I grew up very close to my family and have eight nieces and four nephews. I was very respectful of my parents and their choices.

When my husband and I began dating, his children were eighteen (son), twenty-two (daughter), and twenty-four (daughter) years old. Both daughters were living independently, and his son was a senior in high school with plans for college. My husband kept the kids informed while we were dating, and things were civil. That all ended after the marriage.

His oldest daughter cried loudly through the entire wedding ceremony. Within a few months of our marriage, at a family gathering, she requested details about my husband's will. From there, things have continued to go downhill at a rapid pace. The kids feel that their mom's life insurance should have gone to them. It's two years later and his kids are still angry that their dad has moved on. They are furious that they didn't get to choose how the insurance money was spent. They are very critical of his doing anything new or different, which includes changes to the house that occurred before I came along. We started dating six months after their mom passed away, and I guess they wanted him to grieve longer.

None of the kids live with us now. The middle daughter goes to church with us almost every Sunday, and she and I are growing into good friends. The other two are angry and stuck, making it miserable to be around them. They are unkind to their father and only call when they want money. We sent Christmas gifts to their grandparents' house, but we received no response and they didn't even send my husband a Christmas card.

So my question is, how do we try to mend and blend? Is it possible to become a stepfamily when their hearts are so bitter?

As you can tell from Carol's heartfelt comments, stepfamily adjustments won't automatically be easy just because the children are grown (or due to the death of a spouse rather than a nasty divorce). In some ways it is easier (you don't have to nag a thirty-five-year-old to pick up his socks), but in other ways it can be more difficult because adult stepchildren are invested in the family assets and/or preserving the family name and traditions.

As with younger stepfamilies, the adjustment is often harder when the stepparent is a stepmother as opposed to a stepdad. Stepmothers of both young and adult stepchildren report lower levels of emotional attachment and lower quality relationships with their stepchildren compared to stepfathers. Likewise, children indicate less bonding with stepmothers but report similar attachments with a biological dad and a stepdad.[2] One reason this occurs is the stepmother mandate discussed in chapter 1. Mothers in Western society are considered the focal point for family closeness and emotional connection. Fathers are important but peripheral to the emotional connections in the home. It is less complicated for children to make space in their heart for a "peripheral" father figure (i.e., a stepdad), but to bond deeply with a stepmother is to challenge the biological mother's centrality. This can create an inner clash for children young and old. Maintaining a lower-quality relationship with a stepmother eases this emotional conflict.

You may now be asking, "Is a rewarding journey impossible?" No. Understanding the territory and the common reasons for conflict makes a rewarding outcome more likely.

ADULT STEPFAMILIES

I learned that although I wanted a close family, not everyone else had that desire. I also learned that the reason my stepkids don't want a relationship may not have anything to do with me. Sometimes children have issues that began long before a stepmom came along. I cannot make the problems go away. I must

let God do his work in them. It's not my responsibility to repair
everything.

                                                    Beverly

Your Next Move

Whether you are currently dating a man with children or are a few years into the marriage, your next move should be to extend a hand of friendship to the adult stepchildren. This advice may seem simplistic, but it's not. Successful stepmothers repeatedly seek to build affinity with stepchildren,[3] even if there is tension between them. Surprisingly, some stepmothers make little effort or quickly quit trying to connect with adult stepchildren. This is particularly true when the children are cruel, resentful, or negative. Instead, continually pray and seek guidance on how to find common middle ground upon which to build or deepen the relationship. And remember: Hurt people, hurt people.

Extending the hand of friendship often means:

- *understanding that you are not a parent.* Smart Stepmoms of adult stepchildren know that they are a parent in name only. Seek the role of friend or in-law until the children invite you to go deeper.

- *reaching out to them, even if they don't reach for you.* "I think she ought to make the first move" is misguided and often causes a standstill.

- *learning the adult child's point of view.* It's critical for a stepmom to have empathy for the feelings adult stepchildren may have toward their biological mother and dad.

BECOMING AN ADULT STEPCHILD

Dan enjoyed a thirty-five-year marriage to the bride of his youth, Barbara. Her battle with cancer was difficult for Dan and their two children; she died when the kids were twenty-seven and twenty-five. Eighteen months later Dan met Cheryl through an online dating service. Though hundreds of miles away, Dan's flexible schedule and above-average income allowed him to visit Cheryl, and they fell in love.

When asked how his children were reacting to Cheryl, Dan said, "Actually, I'm surprised by how okay they are. My son told me he wants me to be happy. I guess that means he's glad that Cheryl and I met." It sounded too good to be true, and it was. Dan got an email from his daughter, Jessica, accusing Cheryl of being a gold digger. Then he received this email from his twenty-nine-year-old son, Eric. It sheds light on the typical feelings of adult stepchildren.

> *Dad,*
>
> *Because I love you and desire for us to have the best relationship possible, before I meet your new girlfriend in person there are a few things that need to be discussed. I was hurt by the way you introduced her to me on the phone last week. You did not ask how I felt about meeting her. Instead, you focused on her concerns regarding me and my feelings. She was worried— what about you? Were you worried about my feelings? I don't know her—you barely do—and I don't care how she feels. I care how my dad feels.*
>
> *Did Grandma date after your dad's death? How did that make you feel? Your marriage to Mom is all I've ever known, and it's hard for me to imagine you with someone else. I don't want you to be lonely, and I don't refuse the thought of her (or any other woman), but your lack of concern for me hurts my feelings.*
>
> *Another thing that bothers me is what will happen to Jessica's and my inheritance when you remarry? Will we watch our inheritance go to your new wife? Have you taken care of us in your will? If not, then you need to. If you decide to remarry, what are you going to do with all of Mom's things? Mom wanted them to go to Jessica and me, not your new wife. How do you feel about that? You need to get organized and take care of your children and grandchildren.*

I feel neglected by you. It's difficult to watch you feel excited about a person you've only known for a few weeks. It seems that you are rushing things with this woman. Mom's clothes are still in the drawers of your bedroom. The house is in chaos. How can you move on so quickly?

I want you to find happiness in your life and your children's lives. Please tell me if you believe my perceptions are wrong. Maybe there are things that bother you also. I'm hoping that this communication will bring us closer.

I love you.

Eric

After reading the email, Dan and Cheryl were confused and distraught. "I thought they wanted me to be happy," he said. "I guess that just meant being happy in a manner acceptable to them." At first glance, Dan's viewpoint that his son was trying to control his life seems correct. But we have to look deeper to really understand.

Part of the reason the email blindsided Dan was because he assumed that his children would be as open to his dating (and remarrying) as he was. They weren't. But then, why should they be? If you thought Eric's email was out of line or manipulative, read it again. It is actually very balanced and honestly expresses the feelings of a son who loves his dad, his family, and the memory of his mother. Strong emotions can cause people who equally love one another to end up with conflicting viewpoints. Such was the case in this instance, because the gain for Dan (Cheryl) meant another loss for his son.

Does the son have an entitlement issue when he assumes that he should receive a full inheritance from his father? Possibly. But then again, shouldn't he be reassured of some provision from his father? Besides, the issue may go much deeper than money. It may be that Eric is worried his deceased mother, and he himself, will be forgotten. It would be wise for you and your husband to understand and appreciate these fears.

ADULT STEPCHILDREN: COMMON REACTIONS AND FEELINGS

Many adult children welcome a new stepmom. However, even those stepchildren may have negative reactions that can cause problems. Following are a few of the common reasons why adult stepchildren may struggle with a parent's later-in-life remarriage. One or more may be present in your stepfamily. We have included helpful solutions and responses that might ease the situation.

Loss and the Fear of More Loss

After losing one parent to death, or the family to divorce, children at any age fear losing what remains. Some adult stepchildren fear abandonment or isolation from their father. When the children must share Dad with you, it means a loss of his time and energy with them. This is especially true if the stepmom has children or grandchildren who also occupy the couple's time. This fear is often expressed as anger or resistance in developing a relationship with you. Lee expressed his deep sadness this way:

I am an only child and my mom died when I was thirty-one. I'm single with no children of my own. My dad and I were always very close. But six months after my mom died he was dating, and eleven months after her death he remarried. He moved into his new bride's house, which is located many miles away.

I cried throughout the wedding ceremony. It wasn't disrespect, but

---

Smart Dating

Time is your friend. A rapid dating-to-engagement period increases the likelihood of resistance and negative feelings from adult children. You may be ready, but remember, a wedding will send emotional ripples throughout the generations. Go slow.

Adult children appreciate being informed about a regular dating partner. Don't keep them in the dark as your relationship progresses. This breeds suspicion and a lack of confidence in your decision to marry.

Also, because your time horizon is different from that of adult children, you may think a long engagement is a waste of time. However, try to balance your desire to move ahead with the children's need to adjust to a changing family identity.

*because I was watching my dad kiss someone new while my
mom lay in her freshly dug grave. It all seemed too fast and
disrespectful to my mom. Everyone was partying and having a
great time, while I was still grieving.*

Another adult stepchild replied in anger to her father's engagement. She believed that her dad and his fiancée were both putting
on a courtship façade that would come crumbling down after a
wedding. Using a guilt trip, and perhaps manipulation, she tried to
help him reconsider.

*Dad, you are NOT being yourself. I know you said that Mom
wanted many things and that you regret not giving her those
things. But she knew YOU and loved you for who the REAL
you is. It's normal to try to better ourselves, but I don't even
recognize who you are right now. I know that you have waited
a long time after Mom's death to date. But I don't think Mom
would say you are making a wise choice to marry and turn your
whole life over to someone you have known for only six months!*

If you and/or your husband are the recipient of anger, resistance,
or guilt trips from adult children, remember, these responses are
probably rooted in fear. Acknowledging those fears and *ministering*
to them can help to ease the tension.

Betrayal

In the eighteenth century Samuel Johnson said, "By taking
a second wife, [a man] pays the highest compliment to the first,
by showing that she made him so happy as a married man that
he wishes to be so a second time." Sounds like a good argument.
Unfortunately, adult children might not see it that way. For some
children a remarriage feels like abandonment and a betrayal to the
biological mother.

This is true in divorce as well as death, in particular if the children see their mom struggling with financial or health issues. They

may have the viewpoint, "Sure, Dad, your life with a new wife has turned out great, while Mom has lost everything." Children are especially likely to have this attitude if their mother is suffering because their father abandoned her or had an affair. If your stepchildren feel that they or their mom was abandoned, encourage your husband to hear their pain and apologize for the role he may have played in the divorce. While you cannot fix these problems, you can encourage him to restore a relationship with his children.

If the biological mom is deceased, maintaining a strong family identity by preserving the family name, keepsakes, assets, and mementos is a great way to strengthen the adult stepfamily. Most likely the kids have experienced a disruption of life's continuity; therefore, any choice by the father or stepmom that jeopardizes the original family structure or values may be viewed as betrayal.

Children can't help but wonder, *How would Mom feel about this?* Lauren commented, "Before my mom died she shared that there was a woman she thought had her eye on my father. Now my dad is dating this woman. I think my mother's comments have influenced my relationship with my dad's girlfriend. Although I want my dad to be happy, it bothers me when he spends time with a woman my mom didn't like or trust."

Be Prepared for Double Standards

"His oldest daughter did not come to the wedding. However, the first weekend after our honeymoon she called and asked her dad if we would baby-sit."

Some adult stepchildren worry that the grandchildren will be slighted when their dad remarries. After a Christmas gathering, one adult son wrote to his father, sharing that all the attention he was lavishing on his new wife was causing the grandchildren to feel ignored.

You spent more time getting to know her children and grandchildren than with our side of the family. Are you ready to love her children just as much as you love us? Are you ready to love her grandchildren as much as you love yours? Her kids still

have their mom and dad to love, support, and give care to them.
We only have you. You are our CORE now.

Note that the root cause of this son's hurt is that he feels the central core of the family is being jeopardized. That uneasiness is sure to prompt negative reactions toward the father and the stepmom. You can't stop someone from feeling betrayed, but understanding the emotions can help you to learn how to respond. If this dad doesn't have a heart-to-heart conversation with his son and work out a way to spend quality time with his grandkids, the fear in his son will eventually turn into jealousy.

Another adult child questioned whether her father—who had always taught her to carefully consider the consequences of her decisions—was now giving sufficient consideration to how this decision would impact his lineage.

The fears associated with betrayal and family loss run deep. If your husband doesn't recognize these issues, it's wise to help him make a plan for how to spend time with his biological family. Grandpa taking his grandson fishing alone, or a granddaughter to a movie, might be all it will take to help the adult stepchildren see that you are not trying to take their dad away.

Jealousy and Rejection

Our first year of marriage was the most horrible year I've ever
spent. I can sum it up in one sentence: "He is my daddy and
who do you think you are?" His girls were so nice to me until we
married and moved into his house. But then, oh my, the claws
came out.

Cynthia

Jealousy is the fear of being replaced. A close cousin to jealousy is resentment and competition. Many adult children who have been the "apple of Daddy's eye" feel replaced by a stepmother. That causes them to compete with you. In the case of divorce, this is particularly true when the parental breakup blindsides the adult children because they didn't know their parents' marriage was in trouble. Left in shock, they may feel deceived. Listen to this stepdaughter's story.

> *Even though I was an adult when my parents divorced, I was devastated. Because I am an adult, everyone thinks I should be happy that they went their separate ways—but I'm not. I don't know how to cope. Everything I believed about my parents and marriage has been shattered. And now I've got to deal with my dad having another wife. The whole thing makes me nauseated, and I cry every time I think about it.*

Whether it's death or divorce that caused a loss for your stepchildren, let's be honest: You are taking their father's attention, time, and energy—and they want it back. This loss results in the children feeling less important and opens the door to compete with you.

> *I went from being an only child to having a stepbrother, two stepnieces, a stepsister, and stepbrother-in-law. The family home that I had always known was cleared out and everything was sold. All of Mom's things were instantly gone. I still miss the companionship and exciting trips Dad and I used to take together.*
>
> *When we do have phone conversations they focus around what he, my stepmom, and her kids are doing. (They live nearby and do many things together.) I am now the outsider in what used to be my own family. . . . I feel incredibly alone.*

Listen to that pain. This dad's remarriage has resulted in a significant relationship distance with her father and has actually made her feel like an outsider. Do you think she is excited about having a stepmother? Will she rejoice that her father and stepmother take the exciting trips together that she used to take with him? How will she act at Sunday dinner, or Christmas and Thanksgiving family gatherings?

Your initial response to this situation may be, "She is an adult; she needs to move on and be happy for her dad." However, criticizing this daughter's feelings and loss won't build a bridge. The stepmom in this situation can't make her stepdaughter accept her, but putting herself in the daughter's place and empathizing with her pain can help.

A Smart Stepmom would say something like, "Nicole, I know you and your dad did a lot of fun things together, and it must be hard to watch another woman step into the picture. I know it can never be exactly the same as before we got married, but I want you to know that I want the two of you to continue to do special things together. As a matter of fact, I noticed in the paper that a local art gallery is having a Monet display next month. I know you love art and so does your dad. Why don't the two of you go?"

As a stepmom, this communicates four things to her stepdaughter:

1. She recognizes her pain and loss.

2. She admits things are different but desires to work on a solution that benefits everyone.

3. She is actively seeking ways that the dad and stepdaughter can stay connected without her.

4. She is not insecure or competing for the dad's time and affection.

Concern About Family Finances

Of all the issues regarding adult stepchildren, finances may well be the biggest problem, in particular when the biological mom has died. That's because concerns over family inheritance and assets are legitimate. A Smart Stepmom knows how to resist the temptation to minimize these concerns or label them as greed. Adult children often have the right to know how your marriage is going when it may impact a college fund, inheritance, and significant family keepsakes. Common questions from the kids might be, "If Dad dies before his new wife, who gets Mom's china, and will my stepmother take the family heirlooms?" You and your husband must be proactive in addressing these matters.

Be sure to revisit your financial arrangements in order to address both your long-term provision for each other and your adult children's financial concerns. In his book *Money and Marriage God's Way*, Howard Dayton, co-founder of Crown Financial Ministries, suggests that couples proactively reexamine financial plans when they marry. It is advisable for you to consult an attorney and financial planner who are well versed in remarriage and stepfamily finances. For example, you may need to change the beneficiaries of your life insurance policies or change the ownership of car titles or deeds to a home or other property. New wills should also be drafted to reflect your changing circumstances.

When important decisions are made, it would be wise for your husband to communicate them to his children. Further, to strengthen your marriage, make an agreement not to discuss finances with adult stepchildren unless both of you are present. Some children try to manipulate their dad into giving them money without the stepmother's knowledge. When you stand together it reveals a unified decision. Undisclosed discussions with children about finances are toxic to a marriage and destroy trust. You are one flesh now. In later-in-life marriages the biblical principle of leaving father and mother and cleaving to one's wife (see Genesis 2:24) also has application to adult children. While still responsible to his children, your husband's first priority should now be establishing strong boundaries around your marriage. To make financial commitments and decisions apart

> **Step Money**
>
> "I did not want a prenuptial agreement. That seemed to me to be a business agreement, not a marriage. But after coming close to a divorce and much discussion with Christian lawyers, I found that resolving these money and property matters with stepchildren before a marriage is much better than trying to do it afterward, when adult children claim that assets belong to them. It did not matter that we had been married twenty years."
>
> Donna, Stepmom

from you is to violate his commitment to "forsake all others." If he refuses to honor you in such a way, a marriage counselor may be advisable.

As a general rule we do not recommend prenuptial agreements, as they may plant seeds of distrust in a couple's relationship. However, a good alternative is what our friend and financial advisor Greg Pettys calls a Shared Covenant.[4] This written agreement is designed for couples whose marriages will form a stepfamily, and it clarifies emotionally charged issues for the couple and their children. You can provide details, for example, of how you and the children will be provided for should their father die and you remarry. Proactively addressing these matters and communicating a provision to the children can help to ease fears often associated with money and inheritance. When advisable, allow stepchildren to contribute to wording of legal documents so they feel some influence over the process. Fears increase when decisions are made in secret.

Discomfort With Displays of Affection

During courtship and the early phases of marriage, adult stepchildren and younger stepchildren alike may reel when they observe an overt display of affection between a parent and a new spouse. Holding hands or a quick kiss may not seem like much, but to a child it represents a shift in their father's affections. This is particularly difficult for adult children when the mother died while enjoying a healthy relationship with their father. It's also particularly difficult for the child whose parents didn't have an affectionate relationship, or whose parents' marriage ended with bitterness and arguing. It's hard for them to watch you take pleasure in something that their mom and dad didn't enjoy. One daughter said, "My dad and his new bride are acting like teenagers, and it's grossing me out."

Therefore, in the early stages of the relationship, measure your displays of affection. It may be wise for your husband to discuss such affection with them privately before they witness it. This gives them some time to prepare emotionally for reality.

Pressure to Bond With the Stepmom

Adult stepchildren, as with younger stepchildren, may resent a parent's pushing or manipulating them into having a close relationship with the stepparent. They desire the freedom to move toward accepting the stepmom at their own pace. When a parent pressures the child to accept the stepparent, it often makes the situation worse.

In chapter 1 we indicated that you cook a stepfamily with a Crockpot, not a blender. The low-simmering heat of a Crockpot allows each ingredient (i.e., family member) to soften when they are ready. As one chef said, "You can't fool food; it's done when it's done." When a parent attempts to force the ingredients into a relationship when they haven't warmed up, it creates conflict.

The average cooking time of younger stepfamilies is between four and seven years. Some adult stepfamilies will take less time and others more. When a strong resistance to accepting the stepmom is evident, try to create indirect connection through a relationship with the stepgrandchildren. Some adult children begin to soften and respect their stepmom because of the way she treats the grandchildren. However, remember any bond with you, even those with the grandchildren, may be viewed as a threat to your husband's former wife. Even adult children will typically remain loyal to their mom and abandon a relationship with you or their dad if they feel she is hurt or angry. To understand why this occurs, please read chapters 4 and 5 on "Understanding His Kids."

Confusion Over Dad's New Energy and Love

Your stepchildren have only seen their father in a relationship with their mother. Marriage changes us. If your husband was generally passive with his former wife because she had a strong, direct personality, his children will recognize that behavioral pattern as normal for him. However, that same man now married to a different woman with a different set of relationship interactions may act differently. In his first marriage he was amiable and flexible; in his second assertive and confident. Because his children only know him as flexible, the "new side of dad" can be judged as phony and inauthentic. The quote from the thirty-seven-year-old daughter who told her dad, *"You are losing yourself in this new relationship. I want the dad I know, not the man you think she wants you to be,"* expresses this dynamic perfectly. She views her dad as altering his personality to accommodate his new wife. Meaningful relationships often require numerous adjustments in our attitudes and behavior. However, to his children, those changes may trigger feelings of doubt or confusion because they aren't familiar.

For example, a child who notices behavioral changes in a parent may begin to question the validity of his parents' marriage. "I thought Mom and Dad had a happy marriage. But now I see my father smiling a lot and going out with friends and traveling around the country. He didn't used to like these things before—maybe he and Mom weren't really happy." In the case of divorce, when the children see their dad happy with you knowing he was miserable with their mom, they may blame themselves or feel confused. "You and Mom weren't this happy; was the whole marriage, including having us kids, just a farce? You said the marriage to Mom was a mistake. Was I a mistake too?"

A similar confusion may arise if the relational style of your marriage (and new extended stepfamily) changes the way the original family relates to each other. Family relationships can range from emotionally close to distant. Close families are affectionate, make decisions as a team, and desire to be together often. Distant families value one another but prize their independence. They don't intrude into one another's personal business, and they respect a decision not to attend a family holiday gathering because of personal reasons. If your adult stepchildren have experienced one type of family dynamic, but now that their dad is married to you they are expected to change, they will likely feel loss, confusion, and resentment. A change in how their family expresses relationship creates shaky ground that feels unfamiliar and threatening.

We state again that all of these changes complicate the grief process of adult stepchildren. They may get stuck in a quicksand effect where they rehash the past and desperately try to validate the authenticity of family memories. "I thought we were a close family. What happened?" The answer, of course, is their dad got remarried. *You* happened. If these matters go unaddressed, the stepmom can easily become the target of blame for what doesn't feel safe.

So what can you do? Both you and your husband must acknowledge these unsafe feelings and show empathy for how the changes are creating insecurity. If your husband has never really discussed the divorce with his kids or apologized for the role he played in the marriage falling apart, it's never too late. This is his part in building a stronger connection. Many dads feel extremely uncomfortable discussing the former marriage with the children. But if it's done with humility and compassion rather than bitterness and anger, it can facilitate healing and build a bridge of hope for the future.

The next step is for you as the stepmom to show the kids that you understand the awkwardness. For example, say, "Of course you

> ## It's All in a Name
>
> Initiate a conversation to discuss what terms or names you will use to refer to one another. Find something mutually comfortable.
>
> • Don't insist they use terms of endearment for you (e.g., "Mom"), but if both of you are comfortable, that's fine.
>
> • Discuss how you will introduce each other in public (e.g., "This is my husband's son, Mark" or "This is my stepmother-in-law.").
>
> • Discuss what names you will encourage grandchildren to use. Young stepgrandchildren may use uncomplicated terms of endearment since they bond more quickly. But if "Grandma" feels awkward to the adult stepchild (grandchild's parent), find a variation that suits everyone (e.g., "Nana Rose").

feel strange coming to my house for Thanksgiving. My children and extended family are a crazy bunch of pranksters who hug and hang all over each other. I realize that your father wasn't like that and you aren't very comfortable in this kind of family environment. Please know we don't expect you to act like my family does. I certainly don't think any less of you because our styles are different; I just hope you can put up with us till you get to know us a little more" (smile).

The Desire for Dad

Adult children who have a good relationship with their dad usually want to maintain the relationship after his remarriage. Those with a poor connection may desire to see the relationship improve. Knowing your husband's history with his children is vitally important. Research confirms that your relationship with his children will likely ride the wave of what they established with him before you entered the picture. If the dad has a healthy relationship with his children, there is a stronger chance of the stepmom having one as well. If his rapport with them is weak, most likely you will experience more negative responses than positive ones.[5]

In addition, widowed fathers tend to have a closer bond with the children than divorced dads. This often creates a better atmosphere for a good connection between the stepmom and adult stepchildren (unless his new marriage causes him to lose a relationship with the kids). Over time a divorce can often weaken a father's

Preparing for the Wedding

A wise dad will engage his kids in conversation before a remarriage. This helps the children anticipate the new family dynamics and changes that may occur afterward. It's a great opportunity for the children to express their feelings or concerns also. Encourage your fiancé to begin a dialogue with his children. We've listed a few possible suggestions:

• Before the engagement: "It's one thing for me to date Anne; how would you feel if I became engaged to her? What would that mean to our family?"

emotional and financial ties to his children. This is true even when the divorce occurs after the children are grown. This causes the kids to have a more difficult time accepting a stepmom. Also note, the children may be resentful and automatically reject you if they view your standard of living as considerably greater than that of their biological mother.[6]

These typical emotions will determine the temperature of your family Crockpot. Understanding and acknowledging the circumstances is the first step to learning how to respond appropriately. Here are a few suggestions.

• Before the wedding: "This marriage is going to change some things for our family. I imagine that you are concerned about my spending less time with you or the grandkids. We also need to talk about your inheritance. What are you thinking about these matters?" "Tell me what I can do to help make the transition easier for you." "What are the important things about our relationship or family that you don't want to change?"

• Adjusting to significant life change requires an ongoing dialogue between family members. Therefore, it's important to keep this type of honest communication going. It provides everyone an opportunity to voice questions and concerns.

SMART STEPS FOR STEPMOMS OF ADULT STEPCHILDREN

1. *Discuss with your husband any negative emotional reactions exhibited by his children.* Acknowledge and encourage their need for a continuous relationship with their dad and family stability. For example, when a child expresses betrayal, anger, or alarm over your relationship, your husband might say to them privately, "Your anger yesterday tells me how much you love me, and it shows me the concern you have for our family. I appreciate that very much. I love you very much too. I can only imagine how my new marriage is causing you confusion. I would love to find ways of honoring you and incorporating this new relationship into our family, but I realize this is being thrust on you. I expect that you are worried how this will affect our relationship; could we get together again to discuss that? I'd like to hear more of what you're feeling."

2. *Listen to negative feelings and reactions with humility and openness.* The worst mistake a dad or a stepmom can make is to imply that the child has no right to feel a certain way. These are feelings, and they aren't wrong. They have the right to feel bad. If you invalidate those feelings with words or body language it gives the appearance of coldness and pride. This prevents you from earning their respect. An adult stepchild should not be allowed to insult, berate, or abuse you. Those responses are unacceptable, and your husband needs to step in and confront rudeness. But if the child is expressing negative emotions, the best response is to listen non-defensively. Express humble compassion and validate the difficulty of this transition. For example, "I can see that you are very worried that your mother will be forgotten. I wouldn't want that either if I were you," or "I know this divorce has been painful for you. I'm sorry you are hurting." Don't respond as a victim who is concerned that the kids will take away your spouse or resources. And understand that even when you behave in a godly manner, they may still react negatively. You cannot heal their pain or make them desire a stepfamily. Your role is to respond in a manner that moves the family toward wholeness, not more turmoil.

3. *Realize that your relationship with his children may mirror the quality of your husband's relationship with his children.* If his relationship with them is negative, or if they have never resolved issues surrounding a divorce, expect a greater level of resistance toward you. Even when a positive relationship exists, adult stepchildren may still experience and express a wide range of feelings toward you. Always look for opportunities to connect.

4. *Encourage your husband to have a strong, healthy relationship with his children.* Even when the kids have a good relationship with Dad, they may feel pushed aside after a remarriage. However, if he spends consistent one-on-one time with his children and grandchildren, it should eventually ease the situation. If his marriage to you results in the "death" of the relationship with them, they will not accept you.

5. *Communicate the No-Threat Message (from chapter 9) to your adult stepchildren as well as your ex-wife-in-law.* Say, "You only have one mother, and I am not her. Please know that I understand I could never replace your mom, nor will I try. I also realize that you may feel confused about my place in your life, and I can appreciate that. I hope that we can be friends, and I'm willing to do all I can to make that happen."

6. *Extend the hand of friendship whenever possible.* Remember, you are a parent in name only. Take an interest in their lives; learn about their professions, children, and hobbies; engage in recreational activities; and try to be supportive of their personal goals and family. If possible live out common values and go the extra mile for them. Treat them as you would like to be treated. The Golden Rule isn't just for kids.[7]

7. *Connect through the grandchildren.* Engaging with your step-grandchildren, who often bond quickly with stepgrandparents, can stir warm feelings for the entire family. If possible, help to reconnect your husband with his grandchildren if they have been distant. Unfortunately, divorced grandparents do have less contact, engage in fewer activities, and are less involved with their grandchildren than non-divorced grandparents.[8] Sometimes the tender touch of a woman can mend a distant relationship. You could be the one God will use to heal the brokenness, which might be appreciated by everyone involved.

> **Money Planning**
>
> Before marriage, ask lots of questions about money, inheritance, and how you will provide for each other should one of you die. One woman shared, "I found out by accident that most of my husband's assets had been transferred to his children; I was so sure I was his first priority that it never dawned on me to protect myself."

8. *Proactively discuss all money matters.* This includes keeping prior commitments that your husband made to pay for college or provide an inheritance. It also includes making sure that you and your minor-aged children will be provided for should your husband die. It is not covetous or a lack of trust to insist on firm arrangements and documents that make your provision certain.

9. *Prepare for holidays, celebrations, and family traditions.* Include stepfamily members along with your relatives for family events. Send Mother's Day/Father's Day cards that reflect a genuine sentiment. Dialogue about transitions: "I realize Thanksgiving may feel different this year since my family is joining us. I apologize if this takes time away from your family. Would you like to plan some special time with your dad and family?"

10. *Work toward clearing the air.* If there have been hurtful words or hurt feelings on either side, attempt to build a bridge of forgiveness and humility. Remember that forgiving someone doesn't mean you automatically trust them. It's okay to guard your heart if you sense that the child doesn't desire restoration. But try to find common ground upon which to build the relationship to some degree.

11. *Be patient with adult stepsibling relationships.* Your children and his children may find middle ground upon which to be friendly with one another. Most likely they will pursue a relationship at their own pace. Give them opportunities to connect, but don't orchestrate getting them together in an attempt to force a bond. Age differences may be an additional barrier. For example, if his children are adults and your kids are teens, the connection may be awkward.[9]

12. *Offer compliments and affirmation to your adult stepchildren.* Over the years your feelings may change, but offering words of encouragement and kindness can go a long way toward building relationships.

When Mom Is Deceased

Celebrate her memory. The paradox is while you keep her memory alive, it lowers the kids' resistance to you and increases respect for you.

• From time to time, ask about their mother and listen to the stories.

• Offer the family time to grieve together (e.g., an occasional visit to the grave).

• Anticipate occasions that resurrect grief (e.g., Mother's Day), and find ways of openly acknowledging the hurt.

• Don't feel guilty if adult children treat you like "the mother they never had." Trust that they are capable of knowing what they need from you.

For further reading on this topic, we suggest *When a Parent Remarries Late in Life: Making Peace with Your Adult Stepfamily*, by Terri P. Smith with James M. Harper. While this book is written for the adult stepchild, it gives later-life couples perspective on what their children are experiencing and how to manage the marital transition. You can also share it with your adult stepchildren. This may stimulate much-needed conversation about the changes in the family.

PRAYER

Lord, thank you for this chapter. It has helped me to comprehend the issues surrounding adult stepkids. Forgive me for the times I have judged my spouse or his kids without taking the time to understand the deeper reasons why they act the way they do. Give me clear thinking and discernment in how to respond.

Lord, I desire to be the godly example for this family that you have created me to be. Your Word tells me that in your power the things you call me to do are not impossible or beyond my reach. I need your help in all of these things. Guide me on when to speak and what to do in each circumstance.

I thank you for all of my blessings, including this family. Teach me to have a grateful heart and to grow in every circumstance you allow. To you be the glory. Amen.

PRAYER REFERENCES

Galatians 6:9   1 Chronicles 29:10–11

Deuteronomy 30:11   Psalm 63:4–6

Philippians 4:6–7

Smart Stepmom Discussion Questions

1. The bulk of this chapter may have caused you to forget the hopeful statement at the beginning: Studies indicate that later-life remarriages can be more satisfying than former marriages. In what way does this give you hope?

2. Do a case study together. Read out loud Carol's story found on page 218. What emotions can you now recognize in her adult stepchildren?

   • How did Carol's stepchildren act as a result of these emotions?

   • If you were Carol, what might you do to cope and respond?

3. What are some principles you have read elsewhere in this book that apply to your family situation?

4. What are some ways you might be proactive in extending the hand of friendship? Share the ways you have already tried this step.

5. Which of the common reactions and emotions of adult stepchildren struck you most? Does understanding these underlying emotions help you determine how to respond?

6. In your estimation, what are significant factors in your relationship with your stepchildren? Are they still harboring hurt due to the divorce of their parents? How have you learned to respond differently to those feelings?

7. Review and discuss the Smart Steps for Stepmoms of Adult Stepchildren (beginning on page 235). Which have direct application to your family? Share what you have found to be helpful and issues that cause concern.

8. In what ways might you communicate with your spouse what you have learned from this chapter?

Chapter 13

Baby Steps: Should We Have an "Ours" Baby?

I wanted to have children of my own with my husband. Being just a stepmother was not satisfying enough; in fact, being a stepmother was anti-satisfying.

Anonymous stepmom

———

Part of me feels the pressure of having a child because I am getting older, and part of me doesn't want to create any more stress in our lives than we already have.

Anonymous stepmom

Whether you've already had an ours baby or are considering it, you may be wondering if there is research that adequately reveals whether adding a baby to a stepfamily is beneficial. The results of social research to date on this subject are mixed; there is no clear answer to this important question. I (Laura) knew upon entering my second marriage that I did not want to add a child to my stepfamily, and my husband felt the same way. But many stepfamily couples ask, "Is it a good idea for us to have a baby together? Will a new child help or hurt the existing family?" The answer is, we really don't know. Some families have a great experience adding a child to the mix, while others incur unanticipated difficulties. Adding another life to your family should be carefully considered.

LASTING IMPRESSIONS

Having a baby changes life in many ways. Some of the lasting impressions an ours child has on a stepfamily are similar to those experienced by a first marriage couple, but some are vastly different. If you are considering a baby, you should know what to expect so you can make an informed decision. If you already have a child, this chapter should provide insight on adding yet another child.

Social science offers limited information about how the birth of an ours baby impacts a stepfamily. Compared to the thousands of studies on children and effective parenting, there is little known on this subject. It remains an understudied aspect of stepfamily life; nevertheless, we'll share some of what we do know.

But your decision to have a baby may not depend on what social science has to say. It may depend more on your faith and an emotional desire to create life with your husband. Consider the following perspectives on both the positive and negative outcomes and pray about your decision.

An Ours Baby and Your Stepfamily

You may have heard the theory that an ours baby helps cement stepfamily relationships.[1] Sounds promising, doesn't it? The hope is that having a child gives everyone someone with whom they can equally relate. As one child said after his new half-brother was born, "At last, someone who is related to everyone." The only problem with the theory is that there is little research to support the idea.[2] Stepfamilies experience a wide variety of emotional and relational changes after an ours baby is born. Some are encouraging and some aren't.

For example, the ours child has a greater chance of bringing a positive impact to the home when these factors are present before he or she is born:

- Relationships within the stepfamily home are generally stable and positive before the pregnancy.

- Children already have a positive relationship with their biological parent and stepparent.[3] When this is the case, half-siblings are generally more welcoming to the new child.

- Stepchildren live with the stepparent (and biological parent) full time (or the majority of the time). Residential half-siblings tend to bond more deeply with the new sibling.

- Children are young in age. Younger half-siblings adjust more easily than adolescent or adult half-siblings.[4]

When these dynamics are in place, half-siblings may consider the mutual child a full sibling, which can bring a great sense of joy to everyone. By contrast, adult half-siblings have widely varying relationships with an ours baby. Some are close and have frequent contact, while others are distant and neutral about the new child. Infrequent contact with the stepfamily, a lack of involvement, and the differences in age-related interests are common reasons for the emotional disconnection between a stepchild and an ours baby.[5]

Adult Stepfamilies

Even when a stepfamily has adult children, some couples decide to have a baby. This wide age range essentially produces two families. Typically, the adult children will find their own path to a relationship with the ours baby if given the time and space to choose their level of comfort and connection.

If before an ours baby is born the relationships within the stepfamily home are generally divided between insiders (biologically related persons) and outsiders (step relationships), a mutual child can bring further division. Children who already feel slighted may feel jealous of the time and attention a new child receives, thereby causing resentment toward a half-sibling. The biblical story of Joseph and his half-brothers illustrates this dynamic. They all shared the same father—Jacob—but ten of Joseph's eleven brothers were born to women Jacob didn't love.

The story begins on the day Jacob was to marry Rachel, his chosen bride. Jacob's future father-in-law, Laban, played a cruel trick on him. Because Laban couldn't marry off his oldest daughter, Leah, to anyone else, he snuck her in as Jacob's bride (she must have been wearing a pretty thick veil!). Can you imagine being Leah? No one wants to marry you, so your father sneaks you into a wedding as the bride of a man who doesn't know you are there, let alone love you? How awful! But Laban's plan worked and Jacob married a woman he didn't love. Later, he was allowed to marry Rachel, the woman he truly loved.

> ### Smart Dating
>
> Having a child before a wedding is unwise for many reasons. First, sexual impurity dishonors God and loudly communicates the wrong moral behavior to other children. Second, having a child out of wedlock facilitates an artificial commitment that often fails later. Third, sex before marriage can blind couples to weaknesses in their relationship. It fools them into believing they have a stronger relationship than they actually do. Honoring God's boundary that sex be reserved for marriage guards you from these dangers.

As Leah shared her husband with her sister, the rejection continued. Her misery became obvious when she had children. The first one she named Reuben, which means misery because, as she said, "The Lord has seen my misery. Surely my husband will love me now" (Genesis 29:32). But Jacob still didn't love her. When Leah gave birth to her next child she named him Simeon (which means "one who hears") "because the Lord heard that I am not loved" (v. 33). Leah had many more children, some by a maidservant in the hopes of winning her husband's favor. But her efforts did not work. It was in this uncaring, insecure environment that Leah, her one daughter, and her eight sons lived until the day that the favored wife, Rachel, had a beloved son, Joseph. After Joseph was born, this emotionally divided family was split even further and Leah's sons resented their half-brother. This resentment brewed until the brothers could no longer tolerate their father's favoritism toward Joseph. When the favored son was presented with an extravagant robe at age seventeen, Leah's sons had had enough. They wanted Joseph gone—dead if necessary—and they set out to kill him.

We are not saying that if you have an ours baby his or her half-siblings will try to kill him or sell him into slavery! However, the point remains: In emotionally divided stepfamilies, jealousy and resentment can occur toward an ours baby, especially when the baby seems to be favored. Let's face it, for a stepmother, which is cuter, a sweet-smelling cooing baby or a wise-cracking teenager with body odor and pimples? One consideration, then, in deciding to have a child is whether the family is generally united or still emotionally divided.

Here is another factor to consider. Being related to everyone puts this child in the center of the family's experience. This *hub* position, as it has been referred to by researchers, cuts both ways.[6] On the one hand, it is a privileged position, and the child gains more attention than the other children (especially part-time children). This affords the child more influence and control in the home. On the other hand, this child may feel a constant pressure to create bonds between family members and ensure that everyone gets along.

One stepmom shared with us her experience as an ours baby. Being equal in relationship to everyone did not impact her life in a positive way. This woman's half-siblings resented her mother (their stepmother) for marrying their dad. Therefore they never accepted her as a sibling in the family. "I never completely fit in," she said, "and I still don't. A few years ago at a family gathering one of my half-brothers said, 'Let's get some pictures of just the original family.' " Again, she was reminded that she and her mother are not considered full-fledged family members. After reflecting on her childhood experience, this stepmom does not want to have an ours baby because she fears the child will go through what she did.

If you decide to have a mutual child, it's wise to refrain from communicating high expectations. This includes telling your biological children, the stepchildren, and the mutual child that he or she will "bring everyone together." If that happens naturally, then rejoice. If it doesn't happen, you don't want any of the children to feel they have failed the family.

An Ours Baby and Your Marriage

Did you know that when first-marriage couples have a baby it reduces their risk of divorce? A child strengthens the couple's commitment to one another. As one woman said, "I don't consider leaving my marriage because there's more at stake now." But there's a downside to having a child as well. Couples in first marriages experience a sharp decline in marital satisfaction during the child-rearing years. It seems the business of raising a child can take away some of the joys of marriage. Guess what? These two dynamics are also true for stepcouples who have an ours baby.[7]

The plus side of having a mutual child is that it can create some protection for your marriage (it lowers your risk of divorce; statistically speaking this is especially true if the child is born within the first five years of the marriage) by strengthening your commitment to each other.[8] One stepmother who did not have biological children before the stepfamily, said, "Now I can't consider holding myself back from this family. I don't feel as free to view myself as outside him and his children anymore. I have my own child to consider."

The negative side is that having a mutual child also lowers marital satisfaction (as in a first marriage).[9] This shouldn't be a big surprise when you consider how much time and energy goes into child care and reorienting life around a child's needs. You could say that losing some marital closeness is a calculated cost to having a child. On the other hand, children are God-given miracles that bless couples with the opportunity to love and be loved in a manner unlike any other relationship. Adjusting to a season of change in marital satisfaction in order to receive the blessing a child brings may be well worth it.

Some stepmoms wonder about how their husband will respond to having *another* child; for her, of course, it is *their* child. This difference in perspective about the child is especially true for stepmoms who do not have their own children. "This won't be his first baby, but it will be mine," one woman told us. "I'm pregnant and already I feel alone. Everything is new for me and I want to celebrate all of it, but he is like, 'Oh, yeah, I remember that.' For some reason we're not experiencing this equally, and that disappoints me." For this woman, the joy of a new child is tempered by the reality of being his second wife. For him the special experiences, even those related to the miracle of birth, have been shared with another woman—the first wife. If this factor is dampening your joy, be careful. A seed of envy can easily grow. You chose to marry a man who already had children. Therefore, fight the bitterness and make a conscious decision to accept that you and your spouse may have different emotional experiences in having a child. That is not to say that you can't share tremendous joy. The focus must remain on what you have in common and the love you feel for the child, not the difference in your responses.

The issue of whether to have more children should be discussed before you get married. He may want more children and you may not, or vice versa. I (Laura) know a single, never married woman who dated a man with kids. When the discussion turned to having more children, the man said, "Absolutely not." This ended the relationship. For the woman it was a deal breaker: She wanted kids. But many women marry a man thinking they will change his mind on this subject. That's a very dangerous and potentially toxic form of manipulation.

If your husband does not want another child and you do, this can create a marriage filled with bitterness and envy. One stepmom had this nagging question: "Since I want a child and he doesn't, why did he have one with his first wife? What makes her a better mother than me?" Her fears led to an unwise comparison with the ex-wife-in-law and the assumption that her husband didn't want more kids because of her. There are numerous reasons why people choose to stop having children. Perhaps her husband fell into the category of people who think bringing more kids into an already complicated situation isn't wise, or perhaps he wanted only two children and he already has them. This woman would be wise to get a clear answer from her husband as to why he doesn't want more kids. If after a season of listening, negotiating, and prayer they decide not to have another child, she will need to release her expectations. If her marriage is going to thrive, she will need to conquer her insecurity, fear, and hope that she can have a baby.

An Ours Baby and Parenting

When a stepmom has her own child, she finally experiences the unconditional love that comes from being a mother.
Anonymous stepmom

Having a mutual child can be extremely fulfilling (this seems especially true for stepmoms who do not have a biological or adopted child). In chapter 8 we provide an explanation of parent-child attachment. That section of the book was written for your husband. During the first read you probably focused on how parent-child attachments are different for fathers and stepmothers. We've reproduced that portion of the chart again on the next page so you can now consider what it would be like to have your own parent-child attachment. This mutually beneficial relationship offers automatic love, grace, respect, and approval between parent and child. Specifically, it is an attachment where you are an *insider*—always.

That experience may appear very attractive because it's vastly different from the stepmother experience. It was for this anonymous stepmom:

> In my opinion the benefits of having my own children versus only having stepchildren are far-reaching. Stepchildren were a big disappointment to me. But biological kids are a heart-fulfilling, life-altering experience. As a stepmother I felt like a bad parent and a constant failure. As a biological mom I don't have to share my kids with another woman. I feel like a success. The contrasts are extreme: Each day I fail as a stepmother and succeed as a mom.

Parent-Child Attachment with Biological Moms

- Quick to offer grace in conflict. Children have a high tolerance for conflict and disappointment.
- "Insider" status. Children view parents as "part of the club" with all the rights and privileges of membership.
- Auto-love. Love for the biological parent isn't decided, it's automatic and deeply felt.
- Auto-approval. This attitude says, "If Mom says it, it must be right" and results in a natural bias toward you. It gives the benefit of the doubt and seeks to justify why you are worthy of love.
- Auto-trust. It is assumed that you can be trusted.
- "My space is your space." This attitude says, "What's mine is yours; you have permission to enter my personal space because you're my mom."

Not all stepmothers will experience the stark contrast in parental fulfillment that this woman did. But for her the biological parent-child attachment was profoundly different from her role as a stepmother. Her comments do highlight another important consideration. When an ours baby arrives, many stepmoms discover a vast difference in affection between the stepchildren and a biological child. The ease of being Mom versus the challenge of being Stepmom can trigger a temptation to emotionally withdraw or create distance from the stepchildren.[10] Communicating a message of rejection to the stepchildren will likely hurt and anger your husband. This reaction can also lay the groundwork for resentment between half-siblings. Resist the temptation to pull away from stepchildren when a biological child is born. It's not abnormal to love your own child more than you do the stepchildren, but each child has the right to be treated equitably without favoritism. Remember the wicked stepmother in *Cinderella*? Her daughters got all the beautiful clothes and trinkets, while the stepdaughter was treated like a servant. Her favoritism backfired, not because it's a fairy tale, but because it's wrong and ungodly.

Once again, however, there is another side to this situation. Some stepmothers share that giving birth strengthens their affections and compassion for stepchildren. After their own child is born, stepmoms who had strained, distant relationships with stepchildren (who perhaps visit infrequently) sometimes feel more secure and have more tolerance during the stepchildren's visits.[11] Another possible benefit is that the stepmom recognizes that all children—even her own—act poorly at times. This can eliminate a judgmental attitude toward her husband, his parenting, and his kids. Experiencing the realities of parenting firsthand may increase humility, decrease negative judgments, and soften a stepmom's heart toward the stepchildren.

STEPFAMILY NESTING

If you are planning to have an ours baby, here are some suggestions to consider for preparation.

1. *Expect ripples throughout your multiple-home stepfamily system.* Some issues can be anticipated, but others may quickly appear. For example, a biological mother who has been uninvolved in her children's lives, or disinterested in your family, may suddenly reemerge after you have a baby. Expecting change will help you cope when surprises arise.

2. *Have lengthy communication with all the children and extended family about how life will change after the baby is born.* This conversation most likely will evolve over time. It's important to address both the practical and emotional changes that may occur. For example, anticipate how your family schedule will

change when the baby is born, plus how the kids might feel jealous that the half-sibling doesn't spend time in another home (emotional change).

3. *Try to keep the half-siblings' lifestyle, visitation schedule, and parental contact relatively unchanged after the baby arrives.* Don't allow the presence of the new child to create significant emotional and psychological costs to the other children.

4. *Trust your intuition.* If you anticipate harsh or negative reactions about a new baby from stepchildren (or biological children), plan carefully how to prepare them. Don't just hope for the best.

5. *Celebrate.* When the children are excited about the new arrival, buy them "I'm the big brother" shirts and encourage a family party.

6. *To encourage the bonding between half-siblings, it's best to orchestrate frequent contact between the children.*

7. *Raise all of the children with similar values.* When half-siblings perceive inequalities in rules, expectations, the availability of money, or affection, they can become jealous and angry.

8. *Refrain from being defensive or easily offended when stepchildren voice frustration or concern over how the new baby has affected them.* If the relationship with your stepkids is strained, you will be tempted to assume every comment has to do with being a stepfamily. Note that older full siblings in biological families commonly voice such concerns as well. My (Ron) sister's three-year-old firstborn smiled, and while firmly smacking his infant brother in the chest, said, "We don't hit the baby, do we,

---

When Mom Is Deceased

Contact the deceased mother's extended family (her parents and siblings), and give them permission to be involved in the life of your child. Their involvement, for example, as "grandparents" in birthdays, holidays, child care, etc., bridges the insider/outsider gap in your home and blesses children with lots of love. Possessiveness divides; permission connects.

When a stepmom encourages bonding with the original mother's family, it reduces the relational gaps between half-siblings. For example, it's helpful when the older children's grandparents provide the ours baby with a gift at Christmas too.

Mommy?" Needless to say, she ran across the room to where they were sitting as fast as she could! Sibling rivalry is normal. Not every expression is stepfamily rejection. And if a stepmom over-reacts, it sends a rejecting message to the children in return.

Marriage Adjustment Tips

1. *Expect that the addition of a child will result in less time for each other.* While it may take a few months before you find time alone, be intentional to carve out time for dancing and dining again soon.

2. *If this is your first child, remember that your husband has been here before.* Don't hold this against him, as it's normal for him to feel less excited about the firsts. You may respond the same way with your own second child!

Parenting Adjustment Tips

1. *Every season of parenting requires couples to discuss their expectations and how they will share parenting responsibilities.* It's possible that if your children and stepchildren are older you may not have discussed how you will raise and care for an infant. Proactively talk through these matters as husband and wife.

2. *As your child enters the world, take note of your feelings toward your stepchildren.* It's not uncommon to have differing emotions, but be careful to treat the children equally. Guard against pulling away from his children—connecting with your own child is going to be easier.

3. *Fathers should strive to invest themselves equally in all their children, even if they feel guilty for having more time with the ours child.* It's normal for a dad to desire more time with a baby who doesn't have an ex-wife attached. Help your husband to remember that it's wise for him to stay connected with his older kids.

SO WHAT SHOULD YOU DO?

It's obvious that we can't tell you whether you should or should not have an ours baby. It's tremendously complicated, and there isn't a solid way to predict the outcome or the impact on everyone involved. However, one thing is vitally important: Examine your motives and your expectations, and be certain that having a child is not part of an unrealistic fantasy or an effort to control and/or create family harmony. It is unfair to burden an infant with that role. In addition, if your desire to have a child is an attempt to lure your husband away from his other children or to prove that your child is better than his kids, these motives are wrong and destructive. Thoroughly evaluate your reasons for wanting a child. It's possible that the loneliness and isolation of being a stepmom, plus being wounded by his kids, can ignite a desire for a child. That response to pain is not the proper reason to bring a new life into the world.

Make this important decision based on love, the desire to raise a child, and the Lord's leading. Consider the possible effects on the lives of your kids, his kids, and the ours baby. Pray together and ask God for guidance. He is faithful even when life is complicated.

PRAYER

Heavenly Father,

You are the creator of life. All living, breathing things come directly by your command. It is my desire to honor you by seeking your will in this decision. I know my husband and I can't predict the outcome if we decide to have a child together. What I do know is that I desire to teach all of our children how to know you in a powerful way and to walk with you eternally. Please cover and protect our home with your salvation. I pray that each child, both those who are already living and those who are yet to be born, will know you as their Savior and Lord.

Lord, the kids in our family have already been through a great deal of stress and change. If another baby would make life harder for them, then I'm willing to sacrifice my wants and desires to protect them. However, if it might create more stability, then I want to be open to that possibility.

Lord, my husband and I need your wisdom, guidance, and direction on this issue. Show us what to do. We desire to seek you in all things because you are the Wonderful Counselor and the Prince of Peace. Amen.

PRAYER REFERENCES

Isaiah 40:28   *Philippians 2:4–6*

Proverbs 15:33   *Deuteronomy 5:29; 11:18–20*

Smart Stepmom Discussion Questions

1. How might (have) the realities of having a baby in a stepfamily be (been) different from the motherhood fantasy you had when you were younger?

2. The chapter explains that there is no research to show whether or not having an ours baby is a good idea. Having children is a question of faith and the desire of the couple. Does this create insecurity or fear for you?

3. React to this quote from the beginning of the chapter: "I wanted to have children of my own with my husband. Being just a stepmother was not satisfying enough; in fact, being a stepmother was anti-satisfying." In what ways can you relate to this statement?

4. After reading this chapter and recognizing that another child can be either added stress or a bonding experience, are you more or less optimistic about the impact of an ours baby? Explain. (If you are not interested in having another child, what would you tell a friend who is?)

5. What specific factors give you hope that an ours baby is/would be a good option for your family? What factors cause you to feel apprehensive?

6. Married couples in original families and stepfamilies alike go through many adjustments when a child is born. What intentional steps could you take to protect your marriage during the transition?

7. If the relationship with your stepchildren is radically different from the one with the ours baby, is your husband aware of it? What struggles do you have in communicating your feelings to him?

8. In your home are there differences in the ways the stepchildren and the ours child are parented? What is preventing you and your husband from treating them equitably?

9. What concrete action steps has this chapter encouraged you to take?

Chapter 14

Smart Love

It's been a tough road, and I've made many mistakes. I've cried, I've been angry, and I've wanted to give up. But God has been faithful and kept his promises. Today, our marriage is on the upswing. We've grown, learned a lot, and developed a very deep, loving relationship in spite of the troubles of the step world.
A Smart Stepmom

Because I (Laura) know my flaws and the times I have failed as a stepmom, I was astonished when my stepson Todd recently wrote this to me: "You took Scott and me in as if we were your own, and you never showed us anything but love. I know that wasn't easy because my brother and I were a handful at times. You are very loving to everyone you meet, which may be the reason you are different than the stereotypical stepmom. You have loved us as if we were your own kids."

I had no idea he felt that way, but it was sure nice to hear. And it helped me to realize that I often criticize myself for the times I respond poorly but ignore the things I've done well. As a stepmom my goal has always been to hold on to God's hope, and I believe my stepsons know my faith in Christ is the focal point of my life. I was honored when my older stepson asked me to sing "The Lord's Prayer" at his wedding to his wife, Julie, and my younger stepson asked me to read 1 Corinthians 13 at his wedding to his wife, Jamie. This helped me to trust that God was using my sometimes feeble attempts to be a loving stepmom for his glory. And that he has my entire family under his watchful care.

HOPE FOR STEPMOMS

Vicky shares her "there is hope" moment:

My husband and I took his kids to a nearby fair. The girls were bugging their dad to buy "Mom" some trinkets, and he was getting mad. Then they said, "Dad, we mean Vicky. She's our mom too, you know."

Tonya shares her victory:

Two years ago my sixteen-year-old stepdaughter, who until then had barely spoken to my husband or me, gave me a card on Mother's Day. Previously she had been extremely nasty, but that day she wrote inside the card, "Thank you for always being there when I need someone to talk to." She even signed it, "Love, Katie." I was in shock. Even though her behavior had been atrocious, she took the time to thank me. It was a big surprise, and much appreciated.

Charles Haddon Spurgeon, once England's best-known preacher, made this comment about going the distance: "By perseverance the snail reached the ark." We encourage you, despite the challenges you face today, to persevere. And if there is one area above all others where a stepmom needs to persevere, it's in prayer. Nancy shares this wisdom: "Keep your mouth shut, your eyes closed, and pray very, very hard."

When I (Laura) have no idea how to handle a situation, God's wisdom triumphs and helps me to remember that I'm not alone on this journey. And neither are you. Hold God's hand with each step, and we are confident that you too will experience hope and moments of personal victory. They may not come quickly or often enough, but they will come.

Here are more words of encouragement and wisdom from seasoned Smart Stepmoms:

> When you get a card or a compliment from your stepchildren, save it and refer to it often.
>
> Janet

———

> The kids are getting older and there seems to be a little more acceptance of me—at the very least they have given in! I think it's because of all the times I obliged their special requests for confetti cupcakes and caramel apples for birthday parties. At the time I never got a thank-you, but recently during a family gathering they commented on my efforts and expressed appreciation. Victory!
>
> After trying to do what was right and keeping my mouth closed most of the time no matter how much I wanted to complain, it is finally getting easier. After five years of marriage, we recently had the best holiday ever. I now have a new hope for our blended family. Having a gentle spirit and depending on God for strength has brought me full circle. He has blessed me.
>
> Nancy

———

> My ability to love my stepchildren with no strings attached is really an indication of my relationship with the Lord. God uses stepfamily life to prune us; as we let go of the control and the need to be loved back, he grows us. I am encouraged that over the years I have mellowed and let go of expectations; this release has spilled over into other areas of my life as well.
>
> Brenda

———

> I still get jealous, I can still be manipulative, I still get my feelings hurt, I still yell, I still feel left out, I still resent them sometimes . . . BUT not as often, not as much, and not lately.

That is God working through me to learn about love, grace, mercy, and compassion. I want to learn how to love better. It's a long journey, and I still love my own children more than I do my stepkids, but I am encouraged that our blended family is far better off today than we were when we started out together.

Beth

———

I guess the rewards are when your stepchild connects with you even in a small way, such as a hug or smile. You learn to take those moments, appreciate them, and tuck them away to help carry you through the rough times. I try to remember that my stepkids didn't choose me. This helps me to be more patient and kind (even when they don't deserve it), plus I want to provide a stable figure in their lives. I want his kids to remember our home as being consistent and loving, even when they don't seem to like it.

Robin

HOW TO KEEP THE MAIN THING, THE MAIN THING

As Brenda indicated above, God often uses family life to teach us important spiritual lessons. As a stepmother, one of your hidden gifts is the opportunity to emulate God's marvelous choice to love. Choosing to love children and extended family that are not your own is an opportunity to let God teach you how to love as the Father has loved you. This is smart love. Undoubtedly, this choice will stretch you in ways never imagined. The spiritual lessons God offers us in family—and stepfamily—are valuable and obtainable as we humbly open our hearts to them.

Author and speaker Mary Southerland summarizes it best: "We convince ourselves that life will be better when we have more money, when we find the right mate, when we get the kids raised or build the right house. We tell ourselves that our life will be complete when our spouse gets his act together, when we get a nicer car, when we get that promotion, when we are able to go on our dream vacation, or when we retire. We keep trying to find joy, contentment and peace in lifeless places and things. Jesus Christ is life. He is Joy and Love and He took our place on the cross. That's why we can give thanks when it seems as if there is nothing for which to be thankful."[1]

To that we say, "Amen."

We hope this book has given you direction and encouragement as you seek victories. Please look through the resource section to obtain other helpful tools as you navigate this journey. We hope to meet you soon at one of our Successful Stepfamilies or Smart Stepmom seminars.

We'd love to hear from you. Share your feedback on this book and/or encourage other stepmoms with your personal stepmom victory stories at *www.SuccessfulStepfamilies.com/go/SmartStepmom*, or *www.TheSmartStepmom.com*. If you would like to learn more about hosting or attending a workshop specifically geared for stepmoms, check out Laura's schedule on *www.LauraPetherbridge.com*.

PRAYER

Dear Lord,

Thank you for providing me with the wisdom and insights contained within this book. I praise you for your unwavering love and compassion toward me and my family. It is because of your daily dose of mercy, grace, and faithfulness that I am not consumed with despair. In this world of uncertainty, the promise I cling to is that you will never, ever leave me.

You promise to be my steady guide when the stepmom path feels unfamiliar and the road looks frightening. I trust you to turn darkness into light, and to make the rough and rocky places smooth. I'm so grateful that you never grow weary or tired of me, Lord. And that you promise to exchange my weakness for your indefatigable strength.

O Lord, how contented I am when I crawl into your lap like a child and allow you to be my everything. Rest and sleep are obtainable when you are my shelter. Help me to remember all of this when I think I can become a Smart Stepmom on my own strength.

Jesus, you clearly tell me that you are the way to find truth and life. You are the nourishment I need. When I cling to you my life thrives, but without you I wither. I choose life. I choose your ways over my own. I want to be a blessing to my husband, my children, my stepchildren, my family, and those that you bring into my path. Teach me your ways, O God—I'm yours. Amen.

PRAYER REFERENCES

Lamentations 5:19, 21–24   Psalm 4:7–8; 28:7–9
Isaiah 42:16   John 6:35; 14:6; 15:4–10

RECOMMENDED STEPMOM RESOURCES
FOR FURTHER STUDY

Bergan, Jacqueline Syrup. *Growing as a Stepmom—with God's Help!* Ijamsville, MD: The Word Among Us Press, 2005.

Goodman, Karon Phillips. *The Stepmom's Guide to Simplifying Your Life*. Culver City, CA: EquiLibrium Press, 2002.

Goodman, Karon Phillips. *Stepping-Stones for Stepmoms: Everyday Strength for a Blended-Family Mom*. Birmingham, AL: New Hope Publishers, 2006.

Kolbaba, Ginger. *Surprised by Remarriage: A Guide to the Happily-Even-After*. Grand Rapids, MI: Revell, 2006.

———

For additional DVD, book, and church resources visit our Web sites:

- *www.TheSmartStepmom.com* or *www.LauraPetherbridge.com*
- *www.SuccessfulStepfamilies.com* or *www.RonDeal.org*

ENDNOTES

Introduction

1. Names have been changed throughout the book to protect the identities of those who have so graciously shared their stories with us.
2. J. Larson, "Understanding Stepfamilies," *American Demographics* 14 (1992): 360.
3. Family sociologist and demographer Susan D. Stewart, PhD, personal communication, June 2009. Also, Susan D. Stewart, "Contemporary American Stepparenthood: Integrating Cohabiting and Nonresident Stepparents," *Population Research and Policy Review* 20, no. 4 (Aug 2001): 345–364. This estimate includes functional stepmothers (i.e., both married and cohabiting stepmothers) of minor-aged stepchildren; adding stepmothers of adult stepchildren could double the estimate. A wide 11–18 million estimate is necessary because U.S. government agencies no longer keep detailed reports of trends in marriage, divorce, remarriage, and stepfamilies (see Susan D. Stewart, *Brave New Stepfamilies: Diverse Paths Toward Stepfamily Living* [Thousand Oaks, CA: Sage Publications, 2007], 15–23).

Chapter 1

1. N. Russo, "The Motherhood Mandate," *Journal of Social Issues* 32 (1976): 43–53.
2. Lawrence H. Ganong and Marilyn Coleman, *Stepfamily Relationships: Development, Dynamics, and Interventions* (New York: Kluwer Academic/Plenum Publishers, 2004).

3. Marilyn Coleman and Lawrence Ganong, "Financial Management in Stepfamilies," *Journal of Family and Economic Issues*, 10 (1989): 217–232.
4. Ron L. Deal and David H. Olson, *The Remarriage Checkup* (Minneapolis: Bethany House, 2010).

Chapter 2

1. Kay Arthur, *Lord, Give Me a Heart for You* (Colorado Springs, CO: Waterbrook, 2001), 42.

Chapter 4

1. H. Norman Wright, *It's Okay to Cry: A Parent's Guide to Helping Children Through the Losses of Life.* (Colorado Springs, CO: Water-Brook Press, 2004), 17–26.
2. See Nancy Marie Brown, "Happy Marriages," Penn State Online Research, *www.rps.psu.edu/0201/happy.html*; see also Paul R. Amato and Alan Booth, *A Generation at Risk* (Cambridge, MA: Harvard University Press, 1997).

Chapter 6

1. Jean McBride, *Encouraging Words for New Stepmothers* (Fort Collins, CO: CDR Press, 2001), xv.
2. John Rosemond. *Parenting by the Book: Biblical Wisdom for Raising Your Child* (New York: Howard Books, 2007), 103.
3. To learn more about how respect motivates a man, we recommend the book *Love and Respect* by Emerson Eggerichs (Nashville, TN: Thomas Nelson, 2004).
4. I (Ron) learned this expression of humility from Dr. Terry Hargrave. I am grateful for his insight.

Chapter 7

1. Research references for this compilation of statistics are available at Successful Stepfamilies, *www.SuccessfulStepfamilies.com/view/376*.
2. Dr. Susan Gamache, "Parental status: A new construct describing adolescent perceptions of stepfathers" (PhD diss., University of British Columbia, 2000).
3. For a complete discussion of these factors, see Ron L. Deal, *The Smart Stepfamily* (Minneapolis, MN: Bethany House, 2002).

4. Ron L. Deal and David H. Olson, *The Remarriage Checkup*.
5. See Hebrews 13:5.

Chapter 8

1. John Bowlby, *A Secure Base* (New York: Basic Books, 1988).

Chapter 9

1. And it extended to their descendants! Much of the conflict today in the Middle East has its roots in this family rivalry.
2. S. E. Weaver and M. A. Coleman (in review). *Caught in the Middle: Mothers in Stepfamilies*. Reported in Lawrence H. Ganong and Marilyn Coleman, *Stepfamily Relationships: Development, Dynamics, and Interventions* (New York: Kluwer Academic/Plenum Publishers, 2004).
3. "Girlfriends in God Devotional," *www.girlfriendsingod.com*, January 23, 2009.
4. Adapted from Milton Jones, *How to Love Someone You Can't Stand* (Joplin, MO: College Press, 1997).

Chapter 10

1. Patricia Papernow, *Becoming a Stepfamily: Patterns of Development in Remarried Families* (New York: Gardner Press, 1993), 381–387.
2. Emily B. Visher and John S. Visher, *Old Loyalties, New Ties: Therapeutic Strategies with Stepfamilies* (New York: Brunner/Mazel, 1988).

Chapter 11

1. To be clear, we are not advocating this but know that this is the reality for many women.
2. Jeff and Judi Parziale, "Step-Christmas," *Stepping Up* 5, no. 10 (December 2008), *www.InStepMinistries.com*.
3. Perdita Kirkness Norwood, "Stepmothers' Countdown to the Holiday Season," *SAA Families* 19, no. 4 (Winter 2000), *www.stepfamilyrochester.org/main/?p=24*.

Chapter 12

1. Kay Pasley, "Divorce and Remarriage in Later Adulthood," *Stepfamilies* 18, no. 1 (1998). Available at *www.stepfamilies.info*.
2. Susan D. Stewart, *Brave New Stepfamilies: Diverse Paths Toward*

Stepfamily Living (Thousand Oaks, CA: Sage Publications, 2007), 197–198.

3. Lawrence H. Ganong and Marilyn Coleman, *Stepfamily Relationships*, 124–125.

4. For more information about a Shared Covenant, see Greg S. Pettys, "When and How to Use a Shared Covenant Agreeement in a Christian Remarriage," *Successful Stepfamilies, www.SuccessfulStepfamilies .com/view/577*.

5. L. White and H. Wang, *Acquiring Stepparents in Adulthood: Effect on Children's Relationships With Parents,* paper presented at the annual conference of the National Council on Family Relationships, Rochester, NY (October 2001).

6. Susan D. Stewart, *Brave New Stepfamilies*, 197–198.

7. Terri P. Smith with James M. Harper, *When Your Parent Remarries Late in Life* (Avon, MA: Adams Media, 2007).

8. V. King, "The Legacy of a Grandparent's Divorce: Consequences for Ties Between Grandparents and Grandchildren," *Journal of Marriage & Family* 65 (2003), 170–183.

9. Anne C. Bernstein, *Yours, Mine, and Ours: How Families Change When Remarried Couples Have a Child Together* (New York: Scribner's, 1989).

Chapter 13

1. Lawrence H. Ganong and Marilyn Coleman, *Remarried Family Relationships* (Thousand Oaks, CA: Sage Publications, 1994).

2. Susan D. Stewart, *Brave New Stepfamilies*, 62–64.

3. Anne C. Bernstein, "Stepfamilies From Siblings' Perspectives," *Marriage & Family Review* 26 (1997), 153–175.

4. Anne C. Bernstein, *Yours, Mine, and Ours.*

5. Susan D. Stewart, *Brave New Stepfamilies*, 62–64.

6. William R. Beer, *Strangers in the House: The World of Stepsiblings and Half-Siblings* (New Brunswick, NJ: Transaction, 1989) and Anne C. Bernstein, *Yours, Mine, and Ours.*

7. Kay Pasley and Emily Lipe, "How Does Having a Mutual Child Affect Stepfamily Adjustment?" *Stepfamilies* (Summer 1998). View at *www. stepfamilies.info/research/finding1.php*.

8. Ibid.

9. Anne C. Bernstein, *Yours, Mine, and Ours.*

10. Susan D. Stewart, "How the Birth of a Child Affects Involvement With Stepchildren," *Journal of Marriage and Family* 67 (2005): 461–473.

11. Ann-Marie Ambert, *Ex-Spouses and New Spouses: A Study of Relationships* (Greenwich, CT: JAI Press, 1989).

Chapter 14

1. Mary Southerland, "He Took My Place," *Girlfriends in God* newsletter, Nov. 27, 2008, available at *www.girlfriendsingod.com*.

ABOUT THE AUTHORS

Ron L. Deal is husband to Nan (since 1986) and proud father of Braden, Connor, and Brennan. Everything else is just details.

Ron is a marriage and family author, speaker, and therapist. He is Founder and President of Smart Stepfamilies and Director of Blended Family Ministries for FamilyLife. Ron is author of *The Smart Stepfamily*, *The Smart Stepdad*, and *Dating and the Single Parent*, and coauthor with Laura Petherbridge of *The Smart Stepmom* and with David H. Olson of *The Remarriage Checkup*. Ron is a licensed marriage and family therapist and licensed professional counselor, who frequently appears in the national media, including *FamilyLife Today*, *Focus on the Family*, *HomeWord*, and *The 700 Club*. He is a popular conference speaker and his video series *The Smart Stepfamily DVD* is used in communities, churches, and homes throughout the world. Ron is a member of the Stepfamily Expert Council for the National Stepfamily Resource Center and is a featured expert on the video curriculum *Single and Parenting*. Ron and his wife, Nan, and their sons live in Little Rock, Arkansas.

For more about Ron and his ministry visit *RonDeal.org* and *SmartStepfamilies.com*.

Laura Petherbridge is an international speaker and author of *When "I Do" Becomes "I Don't": Practical Steps for Healing During Separation and Divorce*. She has been featured on *FamilyLife Today*, *Home-Word*, and *Moody* radio broadcasts. Laura is a featured expert on the DivorceCare video series, which has equipped over 12,000 churches worldwide. She has spoken at the Billy Graham Training Center at The Cove and has taught on divorce recovery at Reformed Theological Seminary in Orlando. Laura and her husband, Steve, reside in Lady Lake, Florida.

For more about Laura Petherbridge and her ministry, visit *Laura Petherbridge.com* or *TheSmartStepmom.com*.

More Stepfamily Help!

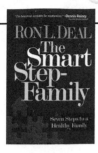

Join Ron Deal as he explodes the myth of the "blended" family. Providing practical, realistic solutions to the issues that stepfamilies face, he helps remarried and soon-to-be married couples

- Recognize the unique personality and place of each family member
- Solve the everyday puzzles of stepparenting and stepchildren relationships
- Learn communication skills to deal with ex-spouses
- Honor families of origin while developing new traditions
- Invest the time to grow their stepfamily slowly rather than look for instant results

The Smart Stepfamily by Ron L. Deal